Project management made easy: the ECCSR approach
by Joe Houghton

First published in Ireland – April 2023
First edition – April 2023
© Copyright Joe Houghton 2023

Website:	http://www.houghton.consulting/pm/
Email:	joe@houghtonphoto.com
LinkedIn:	https://www.linkedin.com/in/joehoughton/

978-1-9162380-9-1   (Paperback)
978-1-916579-00-2   (Hardback)

Joe Houghton has asserted his right under the Copyright & Related Rights Act, 2000 to be identified as the author of this work. All text by Joe Houghton with help from ChatGPT apart from the referenced quotations and other labelled/unlabelled images.

All rights reserved. Apart from fair use in reviews of this book and the associated project "*Project management made easy: the ECCSR approach*", no part of this publication may be reproduced, stored in a retrieval system, or transmitted in any form or by any means without the prior written permission of the publisher, nor be otherwise circulated in any form of binding or cover other than that in which it is published and without a similar condition being imposed on the subsequent purchaser.

Any review should link to: http://www.houghton.consulting/pm/

Project Management made easy…

Dedication

This one is for Tim Sly, the best manager I ever had the privilege to learn from. My project management career was built on his example – thanks Tim!

Project Management made easy...

1 Table of Contents

1	TABLE OF CONTENTS	3
2	WHY YOU SHOULD READ THIS BOOK – AND WHY I WROTE IT	10
2.1	Why I wrote it	11
2.2	How I wrote the book	12
2.3	How to contact me	14
2.4	My other books	15
3	INTRODUCTION TO PROJECT MANAGEMENT	17
3.1	What is a project?	18
3.1.1	So what IS a project?	18
3.1.2	Key components of a project	18
3.1.3	Roles and responsibilities in project management	19
3.1.4	Essential skills for project managers	20
3.2	The Importance of Project Management	22
3.3	Types of Projects	23
3.4	The Project Management Life Cycle	24
3.5	Waterfall	25
3.6	Agile methodology in brief	27
3.7	A basic glossary of PM terms	28
4	THE ESSCR FRAMEWORK	33
4.1	Ethical	34
4.2	Project Management in 1 page (created with Chatmind.tech)	36
4.3	Collaboration	37
4.4	Creating	39
4.5	Sustainable	41
4.5.1	Sustainable Project Management	42
4.6	Results	45
5	RUNNING AN EVENT – CASE STUDY	47
5.1	The Sales Conference - Project outline	48
6	GETTING STARTED ON YOUR PROJECT	49

6.1	**What will we deliver?**	**50**
6.1.1	*The Sales Conference - Deliverables*	*50*
6.2	**The Iron Triangle**	**51**
6.2.1	*The Sales Conference – Iron Triangle*	*53*
6.3	**The 3 Yes's and a No conversation**	**54**
6.4	**Some useful websites for project templates**	**56**
6.4.1	*ProjectManager.com*	*56*
6.4.2	*Template.net*	*56*
6.4.3	*ProjectManagement.com*	*56*
6.4.4	*Wrike*	*57*
6.5	**Project Stakeholders**	**58**
6.5.1	*With, or for?*	*59*
6.5.2	*Equality*	*59*
6.5.3	*Diversity*	*61*
6.5.4	*Neurodiversity*	*63*
6.5.5	*Inclusion*	*65*
6.5.6	*Example EDI Policy*	*67*
6.5.7	*The Sales Conference - Stakeholders*	*71*
6.6	**Feasibility Study – should we do this project?**	**73**
6.6.1	*Define the project scope*	*73*
6.6.2	*Conduct a market analysis*	*73*
6.6.3	*Perform a technical analysis*	*73*
6.6.4	*Perform a financial analysis*	*73*
6.6.5	*Conduct a risk analysis*	*73*
6.6.6	*Determine the first cut project timeline*	*74*
6.6.7	*Develop the overall project plan*	*74*
6.6.8	*The Sales Conference - Feasibility Study*	*75*
6.7	**Developing the business case**	**76**
6.7.1	*Steps to create a business case*	*76*
6.7.2	*Sample business case structure*	*77*
6.7.3	*Benefits of having a good business case*	*78*
6.8	**Project Charter**	**80**
6.8.1	*The Sales Conference – Project Charter*	*81*
6.9	**Sustainability**	**82**
6.9.1	*The Sales Conference - Sustainability*	*83*
6.10	**Ethics**	**85**
6.10.1	*The Sales Conference - Ethics*	*86*
7	**PROJECT PLANNING**	**87**
7.1	**Applying ECCSR to the planning phase**	**88**
7.1.1	*The Global Reporting Initiative (GRI)*	*90*
7.2	**Creating a Project Plan**	**91**

7.3	Work Breakdown Structure – What needs to be done	94
7.3.1	WBS Tools	96
7.3.2	The Sales Conference - WBS	101
7.4	Resource Planning	102
7.5	Risk Management Planning	104
7.5.1	Steps for Conducting an Effective Risk Management Analysis	104
7.5.2	The Risk recipe	105
7.5.3	Identify potential risks	105
7.5.4	PESTEL	106
7.5.5	The SWOT tool	107
7.5.6	Assess the likelihood and impact of each risk	108
7.5.7	Develop risk mitigation strategies	109
7.5.8	Implement risk mitigation strategies	110
7.5.9	Monitor and review risks	110
7.5.10	The Sales Conference - Risks	110
7.6	Some risk examples in business projects	111
7.7	Project Schedule – When will tasks be done?	112
7.7.1	The Gantt chart	113
7.7.2	Recommended Gantt chart tools	114
7.8	Finances – how much will this all cost?	119
7.8.1	Budgeting and Estimating Costs	119
7.8.2	Cash Flow Management	120
7.8.3	Financial Risk Management	120
7.8.4	Financial Performance Metrics	121
7.8.5	Financial Controls and Governance	122
7.8.6	Financial Change Management	122
8	**PROJECT EXECUTION**	**124**
8.1	Applying ECCSR to the Execution phase	126
8.2	Assembling your Project Team	129
8.2.1	Define Roles and Responsibilities	129
8.2.2	Foster Collaboration and Communication	129
8.2.3	Build Trust and Respect	129
8.2.4	Develop and Manage Skills	130
8.2.5	Manage Conflict	130
8.2.6	Celebrate Success	130
8.2.7	Useful Resources on team management	130
8.2.8	The Sales Conference - Team	132
8.3	Project Quality Management	133
8.3.1	Define Quality Standards	133
8.3.2	Plan Quality Control	133
8.3.3	Monitor Quality Performance	133

8.3.4	Continuously Improve Quality	133
8.3.5	Manage Quality Risks	134
8.3.6	International Organization for Standardization (ISO)	134
8.3.7	Project Management Institute (PMI)	134
8.3.8	American Society for Quality (ASQ)	134
8.4	**Communication Management**	**136**
8.4.1	Define your project's communication goals	136
8.4.2	Develop a Communications Plan	136
8.4.3	Identify Communication Channels	136
8.4.4	Manage Stakeholder Expectations	137
8.4.5	Monitor Communications Performance	137
8.4.6	Communicate Magazine	137
8.4.7	Harvard Business Review	137
8.4.8	The Sales Conference - Communication	138
8.5	**Change Management**	**140**
8.5.1	Why Change Management is so important in Project Management	140
8.5.2	Minimizing Fear and Resistance to Change	141
8.5.3	Emotional Intelligence	142
8.5.4	Kotter's 8 steps of Change	144
8.5.5	Involving Stakeholders in Consultative Discussions	147
8.5.6	The Necessity for Proactive Action in Managing Change	147
9	**PROJECT MONITORING AND CONTROLLING**	**149**
9.1	**Project Performance Monitoring**	**150**
9.2	**The Project Change Control Process**	**151**
The Stage-Gate Process		153
9.2.1	Idea Generation	154
9.2.2	Idea Screening	154
9.2.3	Concept Development	154
9.2.4	Business Analysis	154
9.2.5	Project Development	154
9.2.6	Testing and Validation	155
9.2.7	Launch	155
9.3	**Irrational escalation of commitment**	**156**
9.4	**Project Risk Monitoring and Control**	**158**
9.4.1	Step 1: Identify Risks	158
9.4.2	Step 2: Assess Risks	158
9.4.3	Step 3: Develop Risk Responses	158
9.4.4	Step 4: Monitor Risks	158
9.4.5	The Risk Register	159
9.5	**Project Status Reporting**	**162**
9.5.1	The 4-box approach – project status on a page	163

9.5.2	Project dashboards	164

10 PROJECT CLOSURE 165

10.1	Applying ECCSR to the Closing phase	166
10.2	Doing a Lessons Learned Review	168
10.2.1	Lessons from the trenches – the After Action Review	168
10.2.2	Start Stop Continue	169
10.3	Project Deliverables Acceptance	172
10.4	Project Closure Checklist	173
10.5	Project Evaluation	175
10.6	Knowledge Transfer	176
10.7	Celebrating achievements & team recognition	178
10.7.1	The Sales Conference - Closure	179

11 KEY PROJECT MANAGEMENT ORGANISATIONS 181

11.1	Prince2	183
11.2	The PMI	185
11.3	The APM	187
11.4	Agile Alliance	189
11.5	Scrum Alliance	191
11.6	IPMA – International Project Management Association	193
11.7	IPM – Institute of Project Management	195
11.8	LCI - Lean Construction Institute	196

12 PROJECT MANAGEMENT METHODOLOGIES.................................. 198

12.1	Useful Resources	200
12.2	Waterfall	201
12.3	Agile	203
12.3.1	History and Development of Agile	203
12.3.2	How Agile Differs from Waterfall	203
12.3.3	Why Agile is Better than Waterfall for Modern Projects	205
12.3.4	An AGILE Glossary of terms	206
12.4	Six Sigma	213
12.4.1	DMADV - a variant of the DMAIC approach	214
12.4.2	Six Sigma resources	215
12.4.3	A Six Sigma Glossary of terms	216
12.5	LEAN	220
12.5.1	The key principles of LEAN	220
12.5.2	Stages of LEAN project development	221

12.5.3	The 7 types of waste	221
12.5.4	Lean Enterprise Institute	222
12.5.5	The Toyota Way	223
12.5.6	The Lean Startup	223
12.5.7	LEAN Production	223
12.5.8	A LEAN glossary of terms	224
12.6	Lean Six Sigma	233
12.6.1	Lean Six Sigma Institute	234
12.6.2	The Lean Six Sigma Pocket Toolbook	234
12.6.3	Lean Six Sigma for Dummies	234
12.6.4	The Six Sigma Handbook	234
12.7	KANBAN	235
12.7.1	Some useful KANBAN resources:	235
12.7.2	A KANBAN Glossary of terms :	237

13 COMMON PROJECT MANAGEMENT MISTAKES AND HOW TO AVOID THEM 239

13.1	Not Defining the Project Scope	241
13.2	Not Managing Stakeholder Expectations	243
13.3	Poor Resource Planning	245
13.4	Ineffective Communication	247
13.5	Lack of collaboration	248

14 LEADERSHIP AND TEAM MANAGEMENT 250

14.1	ECCSR and Leadership	251
14.2	Leadership Styles	252
14.2.1	Transformational Leadership:	252
14.2.2	Situational Leadership	253
14.2.3	Servant Leadership	254
14.2.4	Core leadership styles - Lewin	257
14.2.5	Leadership styles references	258
14.3	Team Building	259
14.3.1	What is a team?	259
14.3.2	Building the team	260
14.3.3	Tuckman's team formation cycle	261
14.3.4	Modern approaches to team building	261
14.4	Conflict Management	264
14.5	Motivation	265
14.5.1	Points of view – the cathedral…	265

15 TOOLS FOR PROJECT MANAGEMENT 267

15.1	Microsoft Project	270
15.2	Microsoft Planner	272
15.3	Gannter	274
15.4	TeamGantt	276
15.5	OpenProject	278
15.6	ClickUp	280
15.7	Wrike	282
15.8	Monday.com	284
15.9	Trello	287
15.10	Asana	289

16 BUILDING A CAREER IN PROJECT MANAGEMENT 291

16.1	Qualifications and certifications	293
16.2	Networking	294
16.3	Tips for landing your first project management job	296

17 SOME RECOMMENDED BOOKS ON PROJECT MANAGEMENT 298

18 CONCLUSION 302

18.1	The future of Project Management.	303
18.1.1	88 million jobs	303
18.1.2	Growth of AGILE	303
18.1.3	Artificial Intelligence	303
18.1.4	Developments in certifications	305
18.1.5	Managing distributed teams	307
18.1.6	New roles and specialities	307

19 INDEX 308

2 Why you should read this book – and why I wrote it

Projects are how we get things done. At home, at work, in our clubs and societies, projects are the vehicles of change that drive stuff forwards.

There's years of practical and academic research proving that using some basic tools and approaches to projects will significantly raise the chance of getting things done right, on time, within budget and to a satisfactory level of quality.

This book explains how projects work – in a simple, no-nonsense way, laid out in a logical order. No mumbo-jumbo, just basic common-sense tools and techniques that ANYONE can pick up and use to get stuff done faster and more efficiently.

Sections are broken down into small chunks showing what you need to know, and not spending lots of time going into minute detail – this book is aimed at the "accidental project manager" or someone just getting started who wants to get a good idea of what they should be doing and how. I've provided a list of bigger, more in depth textbooks on Project Management in the section on page 298 if you are looking for more depth that this provides.

Don't be put off by the long Table of Contents – it's there so you can jump to the stuff you need easily. There's also a comprehensive Index at the back so you can locate & then understand jargon & terminology fast within the pages of the book.

So, if you are one of the many, many people who find themselves running projects without the title of "Project Manager", or the paycheque to go with it, let me help you understand and apply basic PM principles, and get your stuff done faster and better.

2.1 Why I wrote it

I've spent 40 odd years working in, running and managing projects, large and small, for businesses, charities and academic institutions. The first 20 or so of these years were spent in various companies in UK, then European, then global roles, running projects and programmes for multinationals ending up with General Electric.

I've always been focussed on charity engagement, so I've also run many projects for charities along the way, both as a volunteer as well as a member of various Boards in more strategic roles.

For the past 20 years I've taught Project Management after co-creating a Master's programme in Project Management at University College Dublin's Smurfit Graduate School of Business. This has grown into two, with a full-time and a part-time offering, and this year (2023) we are moving the part-time programme fully online.

Alongside my teaching I run a portfolio career with some consulting, training and coaching, with teaching Project Management being at the core of much of my corporate and non-profit work.

2.2   How I wrote the book

One of my passions is technology, and I've always loved gadgetry, tech and computers in general. I started my professional career as a computer programmer and have been scratching that itch ever since!

This book was written on a MacBook Air with an M1 processor – one of the most significant jumps in computer power I'd ever come across in my many years of using personal devices. It's set in 12-point Calibri font and produced in Microsoft Word. Quite a bit of it was written using the Dictate function in Word, and this is something I'm increasingly using when the house is quiet, as it's accurate and quite a bit quicker than me typing manually.

My editing setup is to have the MacBook on the desk with a small stand and then I have it hooked up to a second screen mounted on the wall – a whopping 42" 4k TV that gives me loads of room for opening lots of windows as I do my research.

And for this book, given the recent emergence of a slew of new artificial intelligence tools, I've been playing with ChatGPT, Canva's Magic Write and others to help structure and offer up ideas for the materials within. The tools are amazing even in their early form – generating lists of points instantly that can then be reviewed and expanded upon.

There are a lot of inaccuracies generated by the AI tools at the moment (March 2023) so anything they do return has to be read and edited very carefully, but using the tools definitely sped up the process of creating this little tome! ChatGPT-4 is a huge improvement on the earlier versions, and Microsoft's announcements as I write the book about CoPilot being introduced into the Office suite showing just how pervasive this technology is going to become in all our lives.

Even during the time spent researching and collating this book, new tools and extensions were becoming available, and I installed a number of these as I went along.

One Chrome add-in (Voice Control for ChatGPT) added voice control to ChatGPT, which allowed me to ask questions in a far more natural way than having to type them in and wait for answers.

Installing the free WebChatGPT Chrome add-in gave ChatGPT the capability of accessing current information on the Internet, dramatically extending its capabilities, which up until that point had been limited to returning data based on a 2021 dataset (ChatGPT-3.5).

A key restriction to many of the AI tools at the time of writing this book was the difficulty in citing relevant references, but the WebChatGPT extension overcame this (to a large extent) and allowed me to include up-to-date, accurate and relevant references and links throughout the book. I hope you find these links useful and they are all tested and will give you further backup information.

It's clear that research using tools such as ChatGPT is with us to stay – the trick is to learn how to structure prompts to elicit the information required and then check, check, check to make sure that the text is verified for accuracy.

I hope you enjoy reading it as much as I enjoyed writing it – this book was a really fun exploration into emerging technologies whilst writing about a subject I love – doesn't get much better than that!

2.3 How to contact me

I'm based in Lucan, Dublin in Ireland, and these days mostly offer online services. If I can help you or you'd like to discuss an idea for training, coaching or programme development of any kind do get in touch through any of the channels below – I'm always happy to discuss new opportunities!

- Connect with me on LinkedIn at
  https://www.linkedin.com/in/joehoughton/
- Email me at joe.houghton@gmail.com
- Call me on +353 86 384 3670 – I'm in Dublin, Ireland
- Book me for consulting, coaching or training at
  www.houghton.consulting

2.4 My other books

In 2023 I published the first of the Plus One Education series:

"Innovative teaching with AI: Creative approaches to enhancing learning in education"

Amazon link: https://amzn.to/40M1O2n

"Project management made easy… the ECCSR approach" is the second book in the Plus One Education series.

Project Management made easy...

I've also published 3 books in the Houghton Photography Guides series to date with more in the pipeline:

1. *"Streets of Dublin"* – a guide to street photography
2. *"Take your time"* – the art and craft of long exposure photography
3. *"Picture perfect"* – a beginners guide to digital photography

Streets of Dublin

A guide to street photography

Take your time

The art & craft of long exposure photography

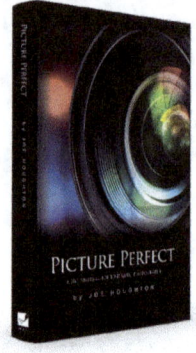

Picture Perfect

A beginnner's guide to photography

All these books are available around the world on Amazon – my author page has links to all the books and can be accessed at:

https://www.amazon.co.uk/Joe-Houghton/e/B07XWQRNJQ/ref=dp_byline_cont_book_1

or via this QR code.

3   Introduction to Project Management

So, let's get started. I've been teaching project management for almost 20 years now and running projects large and small for almost 40 years. For many of those I've been meaning to put together a book on the subject. So this little book is the one that I suppose I would've liked to have when I started project management myself.

It breaks down the topics into manageable chunks, that hopefully are laid out in a logical sequence for most readers to understand.

There is a lot of terminology in project management, just like in any other discipline so there is quite an extensive index to help you locate the parts of the text that explain different terminology.

I've also included a few glossaries of terms for the different project management methodologies, which might be useful as you figure out whether the methodologies are applicable to your projects.

The ECCSR framework is related to each major stage in the project management lifecycle at the start of each section, and there's also a case study running through the book where we look at running an event and explore what might be done for such a project in each stage of the lifecycle.

Project Management made easy...

3.1 What is a project?

3.1.1 So what IS a project?

According to PRINCE2 (PRojects IN Controlled Environments), a widely used project management methodology, a project can be defined as *"a temporary organization that is created for the purpose of delivering one or more business products according to an agreed Business Case"*. This definition is taken from the official PRINCE2 manual "Managing Successful Projects with PRINCE2" (2017 edition), published by the UK Cabinet Office.

I would amend this slightly as follows:

"A temporary organisation created and maintained to deliver one or more products or services according to a specified business case"

The reason for my amendment is that the Prince2 definition doesn't cover services – and the creation and provision of these certainly falls within the output of many projects. And the business only focus is also problematic, as many non-profit organisations also use projects to enact change.

3.1.2 Key components of a project

Now, let's talk about the key components of a project. First, you need to identify the project's objectives, or what you hope to achieve by the end of the project. This could be anything from creating a new software application to building a new bridge.

Next, you need to create a plan for how you'll achieve those objectives. This involves breaking down the project into smaller tasks, setting deadlines for each task, and assigning responsibilities to team members. It's important to be realistic when creating your plan, and to make sure that it's flexible enough to accommodate unexpected changes or delays.

Once you have a plan in place, it's time to start executing it. This involves actually carrying out the tasks you've assigned, and making sure that everything stays on track according to your plan. It's important to communicate regularly with your team members, and to make sure that everyone is aware of their responsibilities and deadlines.

Of course, even the best-laid plans can go awry, and that's where project monitoring and control come in. This involves keeping an eye on the project's progress, and making adjustments as needed to ensure that you're still on track to meet your objectives. You may need to adjust your plan, reassign tasks, or bring in additional resources if necessary.

Finally, when the project is complete, you'll need to close it out. This involves evaluating the project's success, documenting lessons learned, and celebrating your team's accomplishments. It's also important to make sure that any deliverables are handed off to the appropriate stakeholders, and that any loose ends are tied up.

So there you have it - the key components of a project!

3.1.3 Roles and responsibilities in project management

Here are some of the key roles you'll encounter:

First up is **the project manager**. This is the person who is ultimately responsible for the success of the project. The project manager is in charge of creating and executing the project plan, and they are responsible for keeping everyone on the team on track and working together smoothly.

Next, you have **team members**. These are the people who are actually doing the work to achieve the project's objectives. Team members may have a variety of different roles and responsibilities, depending on the nature of the project. For example, in a software development project, you might have programmers, designers, and quality assurance testers.

Depending on the size and scope of the project, you may also have other key roles to consider. For example, you might have a **project sponsor**, who is the person senior management support for the project.

You will also have a number of **project stakeholders**, who are those who have a vested interest in the project's outcome.

End users and/or Customers are normally an essential part of the mix, and best practice has them involved all the way through, from beginning to end.

It's important to make sure that everyone on the team is clear on their roles and responsibilities, and that there is good communication between team members and stakeholders. This can help ensure that the project stays on track and that everyone is working towards the same goals.

So there you have it - some of the key roles and responsibilities in a project. Remember, effective project management requires good planning, strong leadership, and clear communication. By understanding the different roles and responsibilities involved, you'll be better equipped to manage your next project successfully.

3.1.4 Essential skills for project managers

It's a complicated job to do well, so here are some of the key skills you'll need to be a good project manager:

First and foremost, project managers need to be **strong leaders**. This means having the ability to motivate and inspire team members, and to create a vision for the project that everyone can get behind. Good leaders are also able to make tough decisions, and to keep everyone focused on the goals of the project.

Communication skills are also critical for project managers. You'll need to be able to clearly articulate your vision and your plan for the project, and to make sure that everyone on the team is on the same page. You'll also need to be able to communicate effectively with stakeholders and other external parties.

Organizational skills are another key requirement for project managers. You'll need to be able to create and execute a detailed project plan, and to keep track of all the moving pieces that are involved in the project. This means being able to manage your time effectively, and to prioritize tasks based on their importance and urgency.

Problem-solving skills are also essential. No project goes perfectly according to plan, and you'll need to be able to think on your feet and come up with creative solutions when unexpected problems arise.

Finally, project managers need (ideally) to have a strong **understanding of the technical aspects of the project**. Depending on the nature of the project, this could mean having knowledge of software development, engineering, construction, or any number of other technical disciplines.

This last one, however, is not as critical as the others because project managers generally need to make sure that stuff gets done rather than having to actually do it themselves. So if you assemble a good team around you, of people expert in the different areas and technical disciplines, it is possible to run a successful project without being highly technically proficient yourself. There is a higher level of trust needed in these situations, but it's quite possible to run a project without being technically proficient in the disciplines. In my career, I ran many highly technical development teams that created very complex electrical assemblies. I'm colourblind and can barely wire a plug, but that didn't matter because I hired very competent people who could wire a plug and do a lot more. My job was to organise and marshal their various talents effectively.

3.2 The Importance of Project Management

Project management as a discipline is important for a number of reasons, including:

1. **Achieving goals and objectives**: A well-managed project is more likely to achieve its goals and objectives within the given time, budget, and scope.

2. **Effective use of resources**: Good project management helps to optimize the use of resources, including people, time, and money.

3. **Risk management**: Project management enables effective risk management, identifying potential risks and developing strategies to mitigate them.

4. **Improved communication**: A project manager ensures that there is clear and effective communication among the project team, stakeholders, and customers, which helps to avoid misunderstandings and conflicts.

5. **Increased efficiency**: Effective project management helps to improve the efficiency of the project team, which in turn can lead to increased productivity and cost savings.

We'll explore all these and more as we go through the book, but using well known PM tools and techniques really does make a difference!

3.3 Types of Projects

Here are just some examples of different types of projects, all of which fall within our definition from earlier on:

1. Construction projects - building a house, office building, bridge or highway construction.
2. Software development projects - building a new software applications or improving an existing ones.
3. Event projects - planning and executing an event such as a wedding, conference, or festival.
4. Travel projects - Going on holiday, or a business trip.
5. Marketing projects - launching a new product, advertising campaign or market research project.
6. Research and development projects - developing new technology, pharmaceuticals or scientific research projects.
7. Social projects - implementing social welfare, community development, or environmental sustainability projects.
8. Organizational change projects - implementing a new system, process or structure within an organization.
9. Healthcare projects - implementing new systems or processes in a healthcare setting, or building a new hospital or clinic.
10. Educational projects - developing and delivering training programs, educational resources or new school facilities.

3.4 The Project Management Life Cycle

This is just the fancy jargon for the stages that a project goes through. No matter what methodology are using projects need to go through a series of stages to develop and then complete and the PMLC is a term used to describe these stages. In a software project, the development life-cycle is generally known as the SDLC, software development life cycle.

There are various ways to approach a project, but any project needs to go through some basic stages to be set up for maximum chances of success. Waterfall and Agile are probably the most well used of the many PM methodologies and are often used in a hybrid fashion with the "best" bits from each deployed.

3.5 Waterfall

The classic Waterfall model of project management is a sequential, linear process that consists of the following stages:

- **Initiation:** someone starts the project off. This might be from a pain point in the organization, an external force such as legislative change, or just a good idea.
- **Requirements gathering:** The project team works with stakeholders to identify and document the requirements for the project.
- **Design:** Based on the requirements, the team creates a detailed design plan, including technical specifications and system architecture.
- **Implementation:** The design plan is then used to develop the product or service.
- **Testing:** The product or service is tested to ensure that it meets the requirements and specifications.
- **Deployment:** The final product or service is deployed to the end-users or customers.
- **Maintenance:** Ongoing support and maintenance are provided to ensure the product or service continues to function as intended.

In the Waterfall model, each stage is completed before moving onto the next, with little or no overlap between stages. This means that changes to requirements, design, or implementation can be difficult to accommodate once a stage has been completed.

The Waterfall model is often used in projects with well-defined requirements and a predictable outcome, such as construction projects or manufacturing processes. However, it has been criticized for being inflexible and not well-suited to projects with changing requirements or uncertain outcomes. Overall, while the Waterfall model has some advantages, it has largely been supplanted by more flexible and adaptive approaches to project management, such as Agile or Scrum, or hybrid approaches that pull on the best bits from a number of methodologies.

More detail on this in Chapter 12 on page 198.

3.6 Agile methodology in brief

Agile is an iterative and incremental approach to project management that emphasizes flexibility, collaboration, and customer satisfaction. More on Agile later on – see page 201. The following are the key elements of Agile project management:

- **Requirements gathering:** The project team works with stakeholders to identify and prioritize the requirements for the project, focusing on the most critical features and functionalities. This list is called the Product backlog – the list of stuff to be done.
- **Sprint planning:** The project is broken down into a series of short development cycles called sprints, typically lasting 1-4 weeks. In each sprint, the team selects a set of features from the backlog to develop, and delivers a working prototype or product increment.
- **Daily stand-up meetings:** The team holds brief daily meetings to discuss progress, identify roadblocks, and plan for the day ahead.
- **Continuous integration and testing:** The product is continuously tested and integrated with other components, allowing the team to identify and fix issues early in the development process.
- **Customer feedback:** The team seeks regular feedback from customers and stakeholders to ensure that the product is meeting their needs and expectations.
- **Sprint review and retrospective:** At the end of each sprint, the team reviews their progress and reflects on what went well and what could be improved in the next sprint.

Agile project management is highly flexible and adaptable, allowing teams to respond quickly to changing requirements and priorities. It is often used in software development, where requirements and customer needs can be highly variable and rapidly changing.

More detail on this in Chapter 12 on page 198.

3.7 A basic glossary of PM terms

Term	Description
Agile	A flexible, iterative project management methodology that prioritizes delivering small increments of a product or service.
Baseline	The original project plan, including scope, schedule, and budget, against which project progress is measured.
Change Control	The process of managing and approving changes to the project scope, schedule, or budget.
Change Request	A formal proposal for a change to the project scope, schedule, or budget.
Constraint	A factor that limits or restricts the options for a project, such as time, budget, or resources.
Critical Path	The sequence of tasks that determines the shortest time in which a project can be completed.
Deliverable	A tangible or intangible product or service that is the outcome of a project or task.
Dependency	The relationship between tasks where one task relies on the completion or progress of another task.
Earned Value Management (EVM)	A method of measuring project performance by comparing the actual work completed with the planned work and budget.
Gantt Chart	A visual representation of a project's schedule, showing tasks, dependencies, and durations.

Term	Description
Issue	A problem or concern that arises during a project and requires resolution.
Kickoff Meeting	The initial meeting that brings together the project team and stakeholders to discuss the project objectives and establish a common understanding.
Lessons Learned	A review of the project's successes and failures to identify areas for improvement in future projects.
Milestone	A significant event or achievement in the project that marks the completion of a phase or deliverable.
Project Charter	A document that outlines the project's objectives, scope, stakeholders, and authorization.
Project Life Cycle	The stages a project goes through, from initiation to closure.
Project Management Body of Knowledge (PMBOK)	A guide that outlines best practices and processes in project management.
Project Management Institute (PMI)	A professional organization that provides certification, resources, and standards for project management.
Project Management Office (PMO)	A centralized team or department within an organization responsible for defining and maintaining project management standards and practices.

Term	Description
Project Manager	The individual responsible for planning, executing, and closing a project.
Project Portfolio Management (PPM)	The centralized management of multiple projects to align them with an organization's strategic objectives.
Quality Management	The process of ensuring that a project's deliverables meet the required standards and stakeholder expectations.
Quality Management	The process of ensuring that a project's deliverables meet the required standards and stakeholder expectations.
Requirements	The documented needs and expectations of the stakeholders that a project must fulfill.
Resource Allocation	The process of assigning and managing the resources needed for a project, including time, budget, and personnel.
Resource Levelling	The process of adjusting the project schedule to address resource constraints or overallocation.
Risk	An uncertain event or condition that may have a positive or negative effect on a project's objectives.
Risk Management	The process of identifying, assessing, and mitigating risks to minimize their impact on a project.
Schedule Variance (SV)	The difference between the planned and actual progress of a project, measured
Scheduling	The process of organizing and allocating tasks and resources over time to complete a project.

Term	Description
Scope	The boundaries of a project, including its objectives, deliverables, and requirements.
Scope Creep	Uncontrolled changes or additions to a project's scope that can lead to delays, cost overruns, or project failure.
Stakeholder	An individual, group, or organization that is affected by or has an interest in a project.
Status Meeting	A regular meeting to review project progress, address issues, and discuss upcoming tasks and milestones.
Status Report	A document that provides an update on the progress, risks, and issues of a project.
Task	A specific activity or piece of work that needs to be completed as part of a project.
Task Duration	The estimated time required to complete a task.
Time Estimation	The process of predicting the amount of time needed to complete tasks and activities in a project.
Time Management	The process of planning and controlling how time is allocated to tasks and activities in a project.
Triple Constraint	The balance between project scope, time, and cost.
Variance Analysis	The process of comparing actual project performance to planned performance to identify discrepancies and areas for improvement.
Waterfall	A linear project management approach where each phase of a project is completed before moving on to the next.

Term	Description
Work Breakdown Structure (WBS)	A hierarchical decomposition of a project's scope into manageable components or tasks.
Work Package	A group of related tasks within a work breakdown structure that can be assigned to a specific team or individual.
Work-in-Progress (WIP)	Tasks or activities that have been started but not yet completed in a project.

4 The ESSCR Framework

Having run projects for many organizations over 30 years, and created a Masters' programme on the subject at one of the world's top business schools to teach it, I came up with a simple model that I use to ground any project I become involved in.

The ECCSR Framework outlines 5 key areas to address when conceiving, planning and executing any project – Ethical Collaboration Creating Sustainable Results.

Each of the elements are further explored in the following pages...

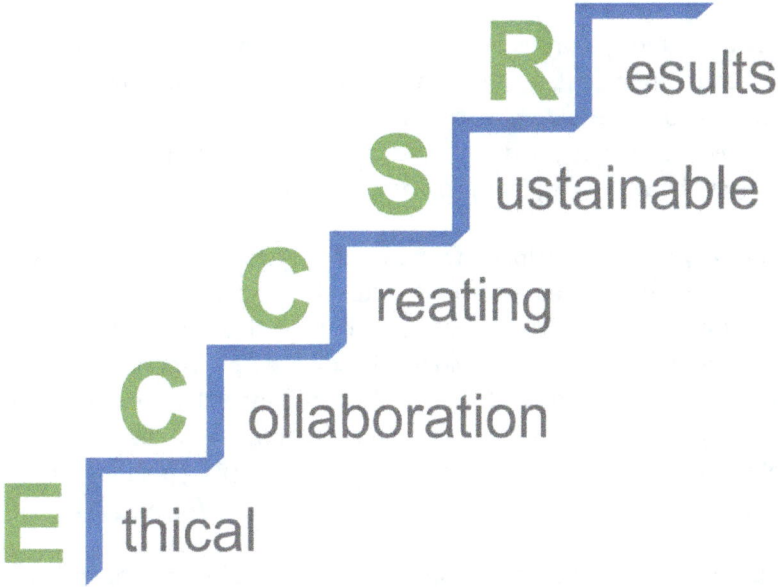

4.1 Ethical

Projects are vehicles of change in a fast paced and pressurised world. Demands are many, time is short, and the lines between what's "right" and what strays into the grey areas or even into outright "wrong" get blurred very quickly. It's critical to have a strong ethical compass, and to ensure that everyone in the project is aligned and signed up to common standards of behaviour.

In the world of project management, ethics serve as a guiding light, helping teams navigate through the complexities of planning and executing projects. By following ethical principles, project managers can ensure that their actions are fair, transparent, and in the best interest of all stakeholders involved.

First and foremost, a project manager should always strive for **honesty** and **integrity**. Being open and truthful helps build trust among team members and stakeholders. Without trust, collaboration and communication can break down, leading to project failure. So, always be honest about the project's progress, challenges, and expectations.

Another key ethical principle is **fairness**. Project managers must make decisions that impact team members, stakeholders, and resources. Being fair means considering everyone's perspective and treating them with equal importance. This could involve distributing workloads equitably, recognizing individual contributions, and valuing diversity and inclusion. As you might know, diverse teams often lead to better problem-solving and higher performance due to varying perspectives and experiences.

Accountability is another cornerstone of ethical project management. It's essential to take responsibility for the project's success and setbacks. By being accountable, project managers encourage team members to do the same, which fosters a culture of responsibility and continuous improvement.

Professionalism is vital in maintaining an ethical project management environment. Adhering to industry standards and best practices ensures that your project is conducted in a professional manner. This includes respecting confidentiality and privacy, as well as staying up-to-date with the latest tools and techniques in project management.

Lastly, **open communication** is a key ethical principle. Encouraging transparency and fostering an environment where everyone feels comfortable sharing their thoughts and concerns can lead to better decision-making and problem-solving. Remember, open communication helps to identify potential issues early on, allowing the team to address them proactively.

4.2 Project Management in 1 page (created with Chatmind.tech)

- Project Management
  - Introduction
    - Definition of Project Management
    - Importance of Project Management
    - Project Management Goals
  - Project Planning
    - Initiation
    - Planning
    - Execution
    - Monitoring and Control
    - Closing
    - Initiation
      - Identify Project Objectives
      - Define Project Scope
      - Develop Project Charter
    - Planning
      - Develop Project Management Plan
      - Create Work Breakdown Structure
      - Develop Project Schedule
      - Develop Project Budget
      - Identify and Allocate Resources
    - Execution
      - Perform Project Activities
      - Manage Project Resources
      - Implement Quality Management
      - Monitor and Control Project Performance
    - Monitoring and Control
      - Monitor Project Progress
      - Perform Quality Control
      - Perform Risk Management
      - Manage Project Changes
    - Closing
      - Obtain Acceptance of Deliverables
      - Close Contracts
      - Conduct Post-Project Review
      - Archive Project Records
  - Project Organization
    - Project Roles and Responsibilities
    - Project Teams and Structures
    - Stakeholder Management
    - Project Roles and Responsibilities
      - Project Manager
      - Sponsor
      - Team Members
      - Stakeholders
    - Project Teams and Structures
      - Functional
      - Matrix
      - Dedicated
    - Stakeholder Management
      - Identify Stakeholders
      - Analyze Stakeholder Needs and Expectations
      - Plan and Manage Stakeholder Engagement
  - Project Control
    - Scope Management
    - Schedule Management
    - Cost Management
    - Quality Management
    - Risk Management
    - Scope Management
      - Plan Scope Management
      - Collect Requirements
      - Define Scope
      - Create Work Breakdown Structure
      - Verify Scope
      - Control Scope
    - Schedule Management
      - Plan Schedule Management
      - Define Activities
      - Sequence Activities
      - Estimate Activity Resources
      - Estimate Activity Durations
      - Develop Schedule
      - Control Schedule
    - Cost Management
      - Plan Cost Management
      - Estimate Costs
      - Determine Budget
      - Control Costs
    - Quality Management
      - Plan Quality Management
      - Perform Quality Assurance
      - Control Quality
    - Risk Management
      - Plan Risk Management
      - Identify Risks
      - Perform Qualitative Risk Analysis
      - Perform Quantitative Risk Analysis
      - Plan Risk Responses
      - Control Risks

4.3 Collaboration

Projects almost always involve many people. Decision makers, workers, customers, those just looking on or wanting a say. Collaborating effectively is key to running a successful project, whether that's how you communicate, or with whom, when or through what media. Putting time and effort into setting up and maintaining effective channels of communications is critical to project success. Let's dive into why collaboration is so important and how it lays the foundation for successful project management.

At its core, collaboration is all about people working together towards a common goal, leveraging their unique skills and experiences to achieve success. In project management, collaboration is crucial because it enables team members to combine their strengths, resulting in greater efficiency, creativity, and productivity.

One of the key benefits of collaboration is **improved communication**. When team members collaborate, they share ideas, feedback, and updates, fostering a transparent environment where everyone is on the same page. This open communication helps to identify and address potential issues early on, preventing costly delays and setbacks down the line.

Collaboration also leads to **better decision-making**. As team members work together, they pool their knowledge and expertise, allowing them to make more informed decisions. This collective wisdom results in a higher likelihood of project success, as potential pitfalls can be anticipated and avoided.

Another important aspect of collaboration is the **opportunity for innovation**. When people from diverse backgrounds and disciplines work together, they bring different perspectives to the table. This diversity of thought can spark creative solutions to complex problems, helping the team overcome obstacles more effectively.

Collaboration fosters a **positive work culture**. When team members support each other and work towards a shared goal, it creates a sense of unity and camaraderie. This positive environment not only boosts morale but also increases overall job satisfaction, leading to higher employee retention rates.

Moreover, collaboration helps to **distribute workload more evenly**, reducing the risk of burnout among team members. By working together and delegating tasks, team members can focus on their areas of expertise and avoid being overwhelmed by trying to do everything on their own.

Finally, collaboration in project management is essential for **continuous improvement and growth**. When team members work together, they learn from one another and share best practices. This ongoing process of learning and refining techniques leads to increased efficiency and effectiveness in the long run.

4.4 Creating

Projects are normally intended to create something – often a product or service. Clear scoping and definition early on are so important to set up any project for success, so clarifying just what the end result should be in terms that everyone is crystal clear about will make your life – and everyone else's – much easier.

Creating new products and services is a driving force behind the ECCSR (Ethical Collaboration Creating Sustainable Results) model and project management in general. The emphasis on creating highlights the need for innovation and the development of unique solutions that cater to the evolving needs of customers and the market.

The importance of creating new products and services lies in the **value** it brings to organizations and their stakeholders. By continuously developing innovative solutions, businesses can maintain a competitive edge, adapt to changing market conditions, and ensure long-term growth. This is particularly crucial in today's dynamic business landscape, where rapid technological advancements and shifting consumer preferences demand ongoing innovation.

The ethical aspect of the ECCSR model ensures that the creation process is guided by principles of fairness, transparency, and social responsibility. This approach to creating new products and services not only enhances the reputation of the organization but also contributes to a more sustainable and equitable world. By prioritizing ethical considerations, project managers can deliver solutions that have a positive impact on society, the environment, and the economy.

Collaboration is also key to **creating innovative products and services**. By fostering a collaborative environment, project managers can tap into the collective intelligence of their team members, leading to a richer pool of ideas and creative solutions. This collaborative approach encourages team members to share their knowledge, learn from each other, and leverage their unique skills and experiences in the creation process.

Sustainable results are crucial in the creation process because they ensure that the new products or services have a long-lasting impact and contribute positively to the organization's success. By emphasizing sustainability, project managers can avoid short-term solutions that may lead to unforeseen problems down the line. Instead, they can deliver outcomes that not only benefit the organization but also stand the test of time.

By incorporating the ECCSR model into your project management approach, you can emphasize ethical collaboration and sustainability, leading to more successful projects and a positive impact on both the organization and the broader community. So, as you venture into the world of project management, remember the importance of creating and the value it brings to your projects and your organization as a whole.

4.5 Sustainable

Years ago this was just a buzz-word that activists used – not any more. Sustainable practice is fundamentally important in all aspects of our continued life – we are rapidly running out of many finite natural resources with our wasteful and profligate practices, and projects are a great way to make a difference by adopting sustainable practices in the way our products and services are designed and delivered.

Sustainability is a critical aspect of the ECCSR model (Ethical Collaboration Creating Sustainable Results) and has become increasingly important in modern project management. Let's explore why it's essential for project managers to integrate sustainability into their thinking and planning processes.

In today's world, businesses are under growing pressure to address not just their economic performance, but also the social and environmental impacts of their operations. Corporate social responsibility (CSR) has emerged as a key business concept, with companies seeking ways to create positive change while still pursuing their organizational goals.

Sustainability, as a part of the ECCSR model, aligns with the concept of CSR. It emphasizes the need for project managers to consider the long-term effects of their decisions and actions, ensuring that the projects they lead contribute positively to the organization, the environment, and society as a whole. By incorporating sustainability into their planning and decision-making processes, project managers can create outcomes that are not only financially viable but also socially and environmentally responsible.

Integrating sustainability into project management offers several benefits. First, it helps organizations **comply with regulations** and industry standards, reducing the risk of legal and financial penalties. Moreover, it **enhances a company's reputation**, as customers and stakeholders increasingly value businesses that prioritize sustainability.

Another advantage of incorporating sustainability is the potential for **cost savings and increased efficiency**. Sustainable practices, such as resource optimization and waste reduction, can lead to long-term savings and improved operational performance.

4.5.1 Sustainable Project Management

Sustainable project management is an approach that integrates environmental, social, and economic aspects throughout a project's lifecycle to minimize negative impacts and enhance positive outcomes for all stakeholders.

Key components of sustainable project management include:

- **Resource efficiency**
- **Waste reduction**
- **Stakeholder engagement**
- **Consideration of the triple bottom line (people, planet, profit).**

Examples of sustainable development and execution of projects in various industries include:

1. Construction: LEED-certified buildings that use energy-efficient materials, renewable energy sources, and green roofs to reduce energy consumption and promote biodiversity.

2. Manufacturing: Lean production processes that minimize waste and pollution, use recycled materials, and prioritize the health and safety of workers.

3. Agriculture: Organic farming practices that protect soil health, conserve water, reduce pesticide use, and promote biodiversity.

The benefits of applying sustainable project management across industries include cost savings, enhanced reputation, improved stakeholder relations, reduced regulatory risks, and long-term business resilience. Challenges can involve higher upfront costs, increased complexity in decision-making, and the need for specialized knowledge and skills.

Case studies and real-life examples of successful sustainable project management include:

1. **The Bullitt Center in Seattle, Washington, USA:** This six-story building, often referred to as the "greenest commercial building in the world," was designed and built using sustainable project management principles. It incorporates features such as energy-efficient lighting, a rainwater harvesting system, solar panels to generate electricity, and a living green roof.

2. **Interface, a global flooring manufacturer:** Interface has implemented sustainable project management practices to reduce waste, lower energy consumption, and increase the use of recycled materials in its products. Through its "Mission Zero" initiative, Interface aims to eliminate any negative impact on the environment by 2020. The company has reduced its greenhouse gas emissions by 96%, water usage by 87%, and waste sent to landfills by 91% since 1996.

3. **Patagonia, an outdoor clothing and gear company:** Patagonia integrates sustainable project management principles throughout its product development, manufacturing, and supply chain processes. The company uses recycled and organic materials in its products, donates 1% of its sales to environmental causes, and encourages customers to repair, reuse, and recycle their Patagonia items.

These examples showcase the potential of sustainable project management to generate positive environmental, social, and economic outcomes across a variety of industries.

4.6 Results

At the end of the day, projects deliver results. Or they should. However, as all the literature shows, there are still an awful lot that overrun on time or cost, or fail to deliver against the promised levels of performance and quality.

This ties back into the start of any project – define it properly up front and the chances of delivering against that clearly defined outcome are dramatically increased.

The ECCSR framework emphasises the importance of achieving sustainable results in modern projects. In this context, "Results" refer to the outcomes and impacts that a project has on various stakeholders, the environment, and society as a whole. These results should be aligned with the long-term goals of the organisation and contribute to the overall sustainability of the project.

In modern projects, results are of paramount importance for several reasons:

Stakeholder expectations: Nowadays, stakeholders, including investors, customers, and the general public, are increasingly concerned about the social and environmental impacts of businesses. They expect companies to deliver projects that not only generate financial returns but also contribute positively to society and the environment. By focusing on sustainable results, organisations can meet these expectations and build trust with their stakeholders.

Regulatory compliance: Governments and regulatory bodies are progressively implementing stricter environmental and social regulations to promote sustainable development. As a result, projects that focus on achieving sustainable results are better positioned to comply with these regulations, reducing the risk of legal and financial penalties.

Risk management: A focus on sustainable results helps organisations identify and mitigate potential risks associated with their projects. For example, by evaluating the environmental impact of a project, a company can take necessary precautions to prevent pollution or reduce waste, ultimately minimising the risks of negative publicity or regulatory issues.

Long-term competitiveness: Companies that deliver sustainable results through their projects are better equipped to adapt to changing market conditions and customer preferences. This approach fosters innovation and continuous improvement, which can help organisations stay ahead of the competition and maintain their market position.

Enhanced reputation: By demonstrating a commitment to achieving sustainable results, companies can improve their reputation and brand image. This can lead to increased customer loyalty, attracting new customers, and potentially gaining a competitive advantage.

Project Management made easy...

5   Running an event – case study

I thought it might be useful to link a real project to the theory and practice is discussed throughout the book, so here's an outline of a fictional event that we can use as a framework to link the different stages of the project and the tools and techniques that you might employ at each of the stages.

This little picture is used every time we have a reference to the sales conference so you can pick them up more quickly when flicking through the book, and here are all the sections where we discuss the sales conference in relation to the subject being explored:

5.1 - The Sales Conference - Project outline - page 48
6.1.1 - The Sales Conference - Deliverables – page 50
6.2.1 - The Sales Conference – Iron Triangle – page 53
6.5.7 - The Sales Conference - Stakeholders – page 71
6.6.8 - The Sales Conference - Feasibility Study – page 75
6.8.1 - The Sales Conference – Project Charter – page 81
6.9.1 - The Sales Conference - Sustainability – page 83
6.10.1 - The Sales Conference - Ethics – page 86
7.3.2 - The Sales Conference - WBS – page 101
7.5.10 - The Sales Conference - Risks – page 110
8.2.8 - The Sales Conference - Team - page 132
8.4.8 - The Sales Conference - Communication – page 138
10.7.1 - The Sales Conference - Closure – page 179

5.1 The Sales Conference - Project outline

You've been asked to organise a sales conference for 100 sales people at a local hotel and conference centre.

The conference should happen in three months' time and run Monday to Friday with people arriving on the Sunday afternoon and leaving Friday afternoon. The sales team can bring a partner.

A series of sales training events will run throughout the week with some plenary sessions and some sessions dedicated to specific teams.

A number of invited speakers will be in attendance at different times during the week and will also require meals and accommodation as well as travel arrangements being made.

The IT team will take advantage of the fact that all the sales people are in one place to spend time updating the laptops of all the sales teams as they attend the conference.

6 Getting started on your project

Steven Covey in his best-selling book "The 7 Habits of Highly Effective People" (Amazon https://amzn.to/3mdGXpB) says "begin with the end in mind". This is a great mantra for starting off any project, and not doing this well will likely spell disaster for your eventual success.

Project scope is essentially defining what you will do, and also what you won't do in your project, and each of those 2 answers is just as important!

Project initiation (as many of the PM methodologies describe getting started) is the first phase in the project management life cycle, and it involves defining the project, determining its feasibility, and obtaining approval to move forward.

During project initiation, project managers work to identify the project's objectives, stakeholders, and scope, as well as any constraints that may affect the project's success. This phase also involves assessing the project's risks and developing a plan to manage them effectively.

Project initiation is essential to the project management life cycle because it sets the foundation for the entire project. Without a clear understanding of the project's goals, risks, and constraints, project managers cannot effectively plan, execute, or monitor the project's progress.

Project Management made easy…

6.1 What will we deliver?

Unless you're a crazy adventurer, when we go on holiday, most of us book a hotel and our transport well ahead. We take time off leaving a day or two each end for preparation and travel. We know our destination, and this informs us on what to pack – for warmth & sunshine or cold and wet (or both if you're in Ireland!).

Knowing where we want to end up in a good level of detail is the same thing in the project, whether this is a corporate project or a nonprofit one, whether it's IT systems change or product development.

Having a clear vision of the end state deliverables allows you to easily create a map and then a detailed plan to get from where you are now to where you want to be .

6.1.1 The Sales Conference - Deliverables

The initial description given on page 47 would be a good start for this clear vision, but would need some amplification around things like the specific presentations that need to occur during the week, when they would happen, and who would be presenting.

Setting up a webpage with details of where the conference is, transport, access and parking, contact details for the hotel and also the conference organisers within your company or make it very easy to maintain and communicate up-to-date information to everybody concerned. There are many tools now available for creating websites as easily as a Word document, one of my favourite is CANVA's website creation tool which enables you to put together the website and publish it zero cost.

Utilising up-to-date technology like this simplifies the experience for everybody and set up good communications flow from the get go.

6.2 The Iron Triangle

The term "Iron Triangle" in project management refers to the three key constraints that impact a project:

1. **Scope (or performance)**
2. **Time (or schedule)**
3. **Cost (or budget)**

These constraints are interrelated, and changes made to one constraint can affect the others. It's generally accepted for most projects that you can have two out of the three but not normally all three at once. So for instance if you want more in scope then you either need more time or you're going to have to pay more money for additional resources. Alternatively if your budget is cut, you are probably going to have to change your scope to allow for less time to complete the project.

The term "Iron Triangle" was first used to describe these constraints in project management in the early 1960s, during the construction of the Boston Central Artery/Tunnel Project, commonly referred to as the "Big Dig". The term was later popularized in the 1970s in the construction industry and has since been widely adopted in project management methodology.

In recent years, the Project Management Institute (PMI) has expanded the traditional Iron Triangle concept by acknowledging the importance of additional factors in achieving project success. The latest iteration of the Iron Triangle, as described in the Project Management Body of Knowledge (PMBOK), now includes quality, resources, and risk, creating a more comprehensive framework for project management.

Quality: Quality has become an integral part of the Iron Triangle because it directly impacts the overall success and value of a project. It refers to the extent to which a project meets its objectives and satisfies the needs of stakeholders. Quality management involves defining quality standards, implementing quality assurance processes, and carrying out quality control measures. By integrating quality as a core component of the Iron Triangle, project managers are better equipped to deliver results that meet or exceed stakeholder expectations. More on Quality Management on page 133.

Resources: Resources encompass the people, equipment, materials, and facilities required to execute a project successfully. The latest iteration of the Iron Triangle recognises the importance of efficiently managing these resources to achieve project goals. Effective resource management involves planning, acquiring, allocating, and monitoring resources throughout the project lifecycle. It helps ensure that projects have the necessary resources to meet deadlines, control costs, and deliver the desired outcomes. More on Resource Management on page 102.

Risk: Risk management is another critical aspect of project management that has been incorporated into the updated Iron Triangle. Risk refers to the potential events or uncertainties that can impact the project's scope, time, cost, quality, or resources. Integrating risk management into the Iron Triangle underscores its significance in achieving project success.

Effective risk management involves identifying, assessing, and prioritising potential risks and developing strategies to address them. These strategies can include risk avoidance, mitigation, transfer, or acceptance. By proactively managing risks, project managers can better anticipate and respond to potential issues, minimising their impact on the project's objectives and constraints.

More on Risk Management on page 73.

6.2.1 The Sales Conference – Iron Triangle

*From a **time** perspective, we have a deadline of three months to organise the sales conference. This becomes a hard constraint because moving the date is likely to inconvenience everybody concerned and also lead to costs from cancellation fees payable to the hotel.*

***Costs** need to be worked out ahead of time, but this should be reasonably simple as accommodation is known from the hotel rates, other costs of speaker fees, travel panda like can be estimated ahead of time and planned for reasonably easily. It's always advisable to have a contingency fund of between 10 and 20% in case of unexpected spend requirements, and the appropriate spending authorisations should be given to the project team, so that delays don't occur seeking approvals to unblock last-minute problems.*

***Scope** is likely to be one of the biggest issues for an event such as this. In my experience, having organised and being part of many such sales conferences, the chance to have the whole team in the same place for a number of days is a magnet for all the departments and managers to seek time with the teams to show off whatever their latest sales related products or services are. Consequently, very careful management of the slots available during the week must be maintained in order to not overload the programme.*

6.3   The 3 Yes's and a No conversation

In my years as a working project manager, I used the iron triangle to great effect. I had the words time scope and cost written on the whiteboard that was pinned to the wall behind my desk. When people used to come in, as they did on a regular basis, asking for small changes or additions to a project I would point up behind me and say "**Yes**, you can have anything you'd like".

They would smile of course, thinking that the request was automatically going to be approved. Then I'd say "*Of course you can have an extra field. Just answer a few questions for me first if you would. So you need an extra field on the screen no problem. That'll need an extra three days of development time so we will need to put the delivery date back by three days. Is that okay?*"

There'd be a frown, and the person asking for the change would think for a moment and then say no, it's not really possible to delay the project implementation date.

"No problem", I'd say. "The answer's still **Yes**. Let's talk about Cost then. We can still get the project done in the time required. We're just going to need to bring in a little bit of extra resource to get the work done so I'll hiring a contractor to deliver this additional work, let's say €1500? If you just transfer that over into the project budget, I'll get it organised and we can put it in the work plan."

Again, there will be a frown and the person would come back with "*Oh no, I haven't got any extra funds - I was just hoping you could slip this in.*"

"Ah," I'd say "well, the answer still **Yes**. So we can't extend the deadline for go-live on the project, and you don't have any extra money. Well, no problem. Can you just have a look at the workplan we've currently got laid out and tell me what I should take out so that we can fit this extra work in?"

Send me another pause. And then the answer would come back. *"Oh no, I don't think this is more important than anything. That's in there already. I was just hoping you could slip this in for me?"*

"OK," I'd then say. "... so we can't extend the time for go live, there's no extra money to pay for additional resource, and we can't take anything out of the already full work plan. Well then, I'm afraid the answer is **No**."

It's amazing how few times you have to have this conversation with people before they begin to get it. If you constantly say, yes to requests for additional things to be included in a project once it started, your projects suffer from what is known as scope creep. This is a horrible way for projects to balloon and eventually die. It shows a lack of clear management and effective decision-making in a project, and is a very common cause for project failure or at least issues in delivery.

Effectively managing scope creep is a key competency for a project manager, and this will often involve you teaching and managing people more senior to yourself or people with influence outside your organisation. However, failure to do this puts additional pressure on you and your team and significantly increases the chances of your project are not delivering on time on budget or to the expected levels of performance.

6.4 Some useful websites for project templates

When you're addressing the planning and execution of any project, you need to create a set of documents to record and communicate all the relevant information. However, you don't have to do this all from scratch as project management has been around for 70-odd years, so there are lots of templates out there that will probably suit your needs either straight out of the box or with a bit of tweaking.

There are many websites that offer project management templates for download. Here are some good options to get you started:

6.4.1   ProjectManager.com

https://www.projectmanager.com/pm-templates

This website offers a range of free project management templates in Excel, Word, and PDF formats, including Gantt charts, project plans, and task lists.

6.4.2   Template.net

https://www.template.net/

Template.net has a large collection of project management templates available in Word, Excel, and PDF formats. The templates cover project planning, tracking, and reporting.

6.4.3   ProjectManagement.com

https://www.projectmanagement.com/templates/

Part of the PMI, ProjectManagement.com provides a range of free project management templates in Excel, Word, and PDF formats, including budget templates, project charter templates, and risk management templates.

6.4.4 Wrike

https://www.wrike.com/templates/

Wrike offers a range of free project management templates that cover project planning, tracking, and reporting. The templates are available in Excel, Word, and PDF formats.

Project Management made easy...

6.5 Project Stakeholders

Effective stakeholder management is an essential aspect of project management.

Stakeholders are individuals, groups or organizations that have an interest in, can affect or be affected by a project's outcome.

These stakeholders can be internal, such as project team members, or external, such as customers, suppliers, regulators, and the general public. Effective stakeholder management involves identifying, analysing, and engaging with stakeholders to ensure that their needs and expectations are understood and met.

The importance of stakeholders in project management cannot be overstated. Stakeholders have the power to influence project outcomes and can provide critical resources, such as funding, expertise, and support. In addition, stakeholders can also have a significant impact on the project's success or failure. Failure to effectively manage stakeholders can result in delays, cost overruns, and even project cancellation. Therefore, it is important to identify and engage with stakeholders from the beginning of the project and throughout its lifecycle.

Effective stakeholder management involves identifying stakeholders and understanding their needs and expectations. This can be achieved through stakeholder analysis, which involves identifying the stakeholders, assessing their level of interest, power, and influence, and determining their expectations and requirements. Based on this analysis, project managers can develop strategies for engaging with stakeholders and addressing their concerns.

Engaging with stakeholders is also essential for effective stakeholder management. Project managers must communicate with stakeholders regularly and involve them in key decisions throughout the project lifecycle. This can help to build trust and credibility with stakeholders and ensure that their needs and expectations are being addressed.

6.5.1 With, or for?

A practical tip that I've used throughout my career to maintain a sense of equality and inclusion in my teams is always to introduce people working on my project meetings as working with me as opposed to working for me.

If I introduce Bill and say *"Bill works for me in the analysts team"*, it immediately creates a sense of hierarchy and somehow puts me above Bill as more important than him. However, if when I introduce Bill I say *"Bill and I work together. Bill is an analyst and he's going to cover the data structures and flows in the meeting later"*, this puts Bill and I on a level as colleagues and immediately shows a sense of respect and equality.

It might not seem like a lot, but the use of language and the way we frame our interaction with colleagues and other people is really important. It can set the tone for the micro culture that you as a project manager have to create and maintain within the organisation that is your project team and wider stakeholder group.

6.5.2 Equality

Equality, as defined in many EDI (Equality, Diversity, and Inclusion) initiatives, is an essential aspect for project managers to consider when building teams, conducting project discovery, and selecting stakeholders. The importance of equality in project management can be attributed to several factors:

1. **Enhanced creativity and innovation**: Diverse teams with equal opportunities for all members tend to be more innovative and creative, as they bring a variety of perspectives and experiences to the table. This diversity can lead to more effective problem-solving and better decision-making.

2. **Improved team performance**: A culture of equality fosters a sense of belonging and respect among team members, leading to higher levels of engagement and motivation. This, in turn, can result in better overall team performance.

3. **Positive organisational values**: Emphasising equality in project management aligns with the broader organisational values and demonstrates a commitment to fostering an inclusive work environment. This can enhance the organisation's reputation and brand value.

4. **Compliance with regulations**: Ensuring equality in projects helps organisations to comply with legal requirements and avoid potential lawsuits or penalties related to discrimination or unequal treatment of individuals.

To ensure that equality is followed and maintained throughout a project, project managers can adopt the following practical measures:

1. **Set clear expectations**: Establish clear guidelines and expectations for team members regarding equality, diversity, and inclusion. Communicate these guidelines from the outset and reinforce them throughout the project.

2. **Diverse team selection**: Strive to build a diverse team by considering factors such as gender, age, ethnicity, and background. This promotes equal opportunities for all and enhances the project team's overall capabilities.

3. **Inclusive communication**: Encourage open and respectful communication among team members, ensuring that everyone's opinions are valued and considered. This can be achieved through regular meetings, brainstorming sessions, and feedback loops.

4. **Training and development**: Provide training and development opportunities to all team members, regardless of their background,

to enhance their skills and knowledge. This not only supports individual growth but also contributes to project success.

5. **Monitor and evaluate progress**: Regularly assess the project's progress on equality, diversity, and inclusion goals. This can be done through surveys, feedback sessions, and performance metrics. Address any areas for improvement and celebrate successes as a team.

6.5.3 Diversity

Diversity, as defined in many EDI (Equality, Diversity, and Inclusion) initiatives, recognises that everyone is different in a variety of visible and non-visible ways. These differences, which may include factors protected by equalities law, should be respected, valued, promoted, and celebrated. Incorporating diversity into team-building, discovery, and stakeholder selection criteria is essential for project managers due to the following reasons:

1. **Enhanced problem-solving**: Diverse teams bring a wide range of perspectives and experiences, leading to more effective problem-solving and innovative solutions. By incorporating diverse viewpoints, project managers can benefit from a broader range of ideas and insights.

2. **Increased creativity**: Diverse teams are more likely to foster creativity, as different backgrounds and experiences can lead to unique ideas and approaches. This creativity can contribute to the success and innovation of a project.

3. **Improved team performance**: A diverse team promotes a more inclusive and collaborative working environment, resulting in higher levels of engagement, motivation, and overall team performance.

4. **Positive organisational values**: Embracing diversity in project management aligns with the broader organisational values and

demonstrates a commitment to fostering an inclusive work environment. This can enhance the organisation's reputation and attract top talent.

5. **Compliance with regulations**: Ensuring diversity in projects helps organisations to comply with legal requirements and avoid potential lawsuits or penalties related to discrimination or unequal treatment of individuals.

To ensure that diversity is followed and maintained throughout a project, project managers can adopt the following practical measures:

1. **Diverse team selection**: Actively seek to build a diverse team by considering factors such as gender, age, ethnicity, and background. This promotes an inclusive working environment and enhances the project team's overall capabilities.

2. **Inclusive communication**: Encourage open, respectful, and inclusive communication among team members, ensuring that everyone's opinions are valued and considered. This can be achieved through regular meetings, brainstorming sessions, and feedback loops.

3. **Training and development**: Provide training and development opportunities to all team members to enhance their skills and knowledge, and foster a better understanding of diversity and its benefits within the team.

4. **Set clear expectations**: Establish clear guidelines and expectations for team members regarding diversity, and communicate these guidelines from the outset and throughout the project.

5. **Monitor and evaluate progress**: Regularly assess the project's progress on diversity goals. This can be done through surveys, feedback sessions, and performance metrics. Address any areas for improvement and celebrate successes as a team.

6.5.4 Neurodiversity

Neurodiversity refers to the natural range of differences in human brain function, encompassing alternative thinking styles such as dyslexia, autism, ADHD, and dyspraxia. Positively seeking out neurodiverse employees can be beneficial in projects for various reasons:

1. **Unique strengths**: Neurodiverse individuals often possess unique strengths, such as heightened pattern recognition, creative problem-solving, or exceptional attention to detail. These strengths can contribute significantly to a project's success by offering innovative solutions or identifying potential issues early on. For example, individuals with autism are often known for their strong focus and ability to recognise patterns (source: https://www.cipd.co.uk/knowledge/fundamentals/relations/diversity/neurodiversity-work).

2. **Enhanced problem-solving**: Neurodiverse teams bring diverse perspectives and approaches to problem-solving, leading to more effective and creative solutions. This diversity can result in a more comprehensive understanding of project challenges and opportunities.

3. **Increased innovation**: Neurodiverse employees can bring fresh ideas and approaches to projects, driving innovation and improving overall outcomes. Their unique perspectives can lead to the development of novel products, services, or processes.

To positively seek out and support neurodiverse employees in projects, project managers can implement the following strategies:

1. **Inclusive recruitment**: Adopt recruitment practices that are inclusive and accessible to neurodiverse individuals. This may involve offering alternative interview formats, providing additional support during the application process, or using clear and concise language in job advertisements.

2. **Awareness and training**: Provide training to project team members on neurodiversity and its benefits, fostering a better understanding and interaction between neurotypical and neurodiverse colleagues.

3. **Awareness and training**: Provide training to project team members on neurodiversity and its benefits, fostering a better understanding and appreciation for diverse thinking styles. This can lead to a more inclusive and supportive work environment for neurodiverse employees (source: https://www.health.harvard.edu/blog/what-is-neurodiversity-202111232645).

4. **Tailored support**: Offer individualised support and accommodations to help neurodiverse employees maximise their potential and contribute effectively to the project. This may include flexible working hours, assistive technology, or adjustments to the work environment.

5. **Inclusive communication**: Encourage open, respectful, and inclusive communication among team members, ensuring that everyone's opinions are valued and considered. This can be achieved through regular meetings, brainstorming sessions, and feedback loops.

6. **Monitor and evaluate progress**: Regularly assess the project's progress on neurodiversity goals. This can be done through surveys, feedback sessions, and performance metrics. Address any areas for improvement and celebrate successes as a team.

6.5.5 Inclusion

Inclusion, as it applies to project management, refers to creating an environment where everyone involved in a project feels valued, respected, and supported, regardless of their background, abilities, or perspectives. It encompasses inclusive approaches to employment policies, practices, personal behaviours, and the management of EDI issues within the context of business goals (source: https://www.cipd.co.uk/knowledge/fundamentals/relations/diversity/factsheet).

Building inclusion into your planning for a project is important for several reasons:

1. **Enhanced collaboration**: Inclusive environments foster better collaboration, as team members feel comfortable sharing their ideas and perspectives, leading to more effective decision-making and problem-solving.

2. **Increased engagement**: When people feel included, they are more likely to be engaged and committed to the project's success, resulting in higher productivity and better outcomes.

3. **Improved team dynamics**: An inclusive project environment can help prevent conflicts and misunderstandings, promoting a more harmonious and efficient team.

4. **Greater innovation**: Inclusion encourages diverse thinking and creative problem-solving, which can drive innovation and enhance overall project success.

5. **Positive reputation**: Demonstrating a commitment to inclusion can enhance an organisation's reputation, attracting top talent and potentially increasing business opportunities.

Practical ways to build inclusion into your project planning include:

1. **Inclusive team formation**: Assemble a diverse project team that includes individuals from various backgrounds, experiences, and abilities. This can contribute to a broader range of perspectives and ideas.

2. **Training and education**: Provide training on inclusion and its importance to all team members, fostering an understanding of how to create and maintain an inclusive project environment.

3. **Inclusive communication**: Establish open and inclusive communication channels, ensuring that everyone's input is valued and considered. Encourage active listening, constructive feedback, and open dialogue to create a supportive atmosphere.

4. **Accessible resources and tools**: Ensure that project resources, tools, and technology are accessible to all team members, including those with disabilities. This might involve providing assistive technology, alternative formats, or additional support as needed.

5. **Flexible work arrangements**: Offer flexible work arrangements, such as remote working options, adjustable schedules, or task distribution, to accommodate team members with different needs and preferences.

6. **Encourage participation**: Actively involve all team members in decision-making processes, and provide opportunities for them to contribute their unique perspectives and ideas.

7. **Monitor progress and address issues**: Regularly assess the project's progress on inclusion goals, identify areas for improvement, and address any issues or concerns that may arise. Celebrate successes and share learnings to reinforce the value of inclusion.

6.5.6 Example EDI Policy

An EDI (Equality, Diversity, and Inclusion) policy applied to a project management team might include the following components:

1. **EDI Vision Statement**: A clear statement outlining the organisation's commitment to promoting equality, diversity, and inclusion within the project management environment. This statement should express the organisation's values and set the foundation for the subsequent guidelines and policies.

2. **EDI Commitments**: A set of defined commitments that detail the specific actions and goals the organisation aims to achieve in relation to EDI. These commitments may include fostering a diverse workforce, providing equal opportunities for career development, and ensuring an inclusive and respectful working environment.

3. **EDI Maturity Model**: A framework that helps organisations assess their current level of EDI maturity and identify areas for improvement. This model may involve a series of stages, with each stage representing a higher level of EDI maturity. The Department of Justice, for instance, piloted an EDI Maturity Model to aid the development of their EDI Strategy.

   There's a good set of publicly accessible EDI Maturity Model resources at https://www.ops.gov.ie/news/Resources/edi-maturity-model-resources/

4. **EDI Perception Survey**: A survey designed to gather feedback from employees and stakeholders on their experiences and perceptions of EDI within the organisation. This survey can help identify strengths and weaknesses in the organisation's current EDI practices and inform future policy development.

   A downloadable copy of such a survey is at https://www.ops.gov.ie/app/uploads/2022/03/EDI-Perception-Survey-DOJ.docx

5. **EDI Policy and Data Checklist**: A comprehensive list of EDI-related policies and data collection practices, ensuring that the organisation is adhering to relevant legislation and promoting best practices in the field of EDI. This checklist can serve as a valuable tool for monitoring and evaluating the organisation's progress in implementing its EDI commitments.

   Here is an example EDI policy and data checklist that can be used in higher education institutions:

   Equality, Diversity, and Inclusivity (EDI) Policy Questions:

   - Does the institution have an EDI policy in place?
   - Is the EDI policy regularly reviewed and updated?
   - Does the EDI policy cover all aspects of institutional life, including recruitment, retention, promotion, and training?
   - Are all members of the institution made aware of the EDI policy?
   - Does the institution have a safeguarding policy in place?
   - Is the safeguarding policy regularly reviewed and updated?
   - Are all members of the institution made aware of the safeguarding policy?

   Ground Rules:

   - Are appropriate ground rules set and communicated to all members of the institution?
   - Do the ground rules cover legislation and policy related to EDI and safeguarding?

- Do the ground rules promote respectful behavior, open dialogue, and a safe and inclusive environment?

Data Checklist:

- Does the institution collect and analyse diversity data?
- Is the diversity data used to identify areas for improvement and inform decision-making?
- Does the institution regularly review and update its diversity data?
- Does the institution collect and analyse data on recruitment, retention, and promotion?
- Are the data collection and analysis methods inclusive and accessible to all members of the institution?
- Are the data disaggregated by protected characteristics, such as gender, ethnicity, disability, and age?
- Are the data used to inform the institution's EDI policy and practice?

Engagement:

- Does the institution engage with all members of the community on EDI issues?
- Is there a mechanism for collecting and addressing concerns and complaints related to EDI?
- Does the institution provide training and development opportunities on EDI for all members of the community?

- Does the institution collaborate with external organizations and groups to promote EDI and share best practices?

- Does the institution regularly review and evaluate its EDI engagement activities?

Audit Framework/Checklist:

- Does the institution use an audit framework or checklist to assess its EDI policy and practice?

- Is the audit framework or checklist regularly reviewed and updated?

- Does the audit framework or checklist cover all aspects of institutional life, including recruitment, retention, promotion, and training?

- Are all members of the institution made aware of the audit framework or checklist?

- Are the results of the audit framework or checklist used to inform the institution's EDI policy and practice?

6. **EDI Training and Development**: A commitment to provide ongoing training and development opportunities to employees and stakeholders on EDI topics. This may include workshops, seminars, or e-learning modules designed to increase awareness, understanding, and practical application of EDI principles within the project management context.

7. **EDI Monitoring and Reporting**: A system for regularly monitoring and reporting on the organisation's progress towards achieving its EDI commitments. This may involve setting measurable targets, establishing performance indicators, and sharing progress updates with employees and stakeholders.

By implementing a comprehensive set of EDI guidelines or policy, organisations can ensure that their project management practices align with their overall commitment to promoting equality, diversity, and inclusion. This approach not only helps to create a more inclusive working environment but also contributes to the long-term success of the organisation.

6.5.7   The Sales Conference - Stakeholders

Creating a list of stakeholders for the sales conference might include the following:

- *You as the project manager*
- *The National Sales Manager*
- *The Managing Director and other members of the senior leadership team*
- *Sales teams and their associated staff*
- *Partners of the sales-people*
- *The hotel staff*
- *Staff in the travel department*
- *External speakers*
- *The IT department*
- *The Finance department*

- Research & development who will probably be delivering some sessions on new or in-development products coming down the pipeline
- The PR department – they'll be handling publicity around the event and the prize-winning sales people and teams
- Purchasing – to buy prizes for the sales people, swag bag stuff for the conference, and gifts for speakers
- External IT providers to provide the screens, audio, recording and stage effects

Wherever possible, your stakeholders should be listed by name in a spreadsheet or database, and then their contact details, email address and other information about them recorded in a way that is accessible to the whole project team.

Something like a Google sheet can be a great way of keeping a single set of information about your project stakeholders that can be accessed and updated by any member of the project team at any time and keep a single point of up-to-date information that everybody can work off.

6.6 Feasibility Study – should we do this project?

Creating a feasibility study is an essential step in project management as it helps to determine whether a project is viable and achievable. Here is an outline of the process of creating a typical feasibility study:

6.6.1 Define the project scope

The first step in creating a feasibility study is to define the project's scope, including its objectives, deliverables, and key stakeholders. This will help to determine the project's overall purpose and what it aims to achieve.

6.6.2 Conduct a market analysis

Conducting a market analysis involves researching the project's target market, including its size, competition, and growth potential. This analysis helps to determine whether the project is likely to be successful in the market.

6.6.3 Perform a technical analysis

The technical analysis involves assessing the project's technical feasibility, including its design, development, and implementation requirements. This analysis helps to determine whether the project can be technically achieved.

6.6.4 Perform a financial analysis

The financial analysis involves assessing the project's financial feasibility, including its costs, revenue, and profitability. This analysis helps to determine whether the project is financially viable and whether it can generate sufficient returns on investment.

6.6.5 Conduct a risk analysis

The risk analysis involves identifying and assessing the project's risks, including potential issues that could impact the project's success. This analysis helps to determine the project's risk level and to develop strategies to mitigate potential risks.

6.6.6 Determine the first cut project timeline

The project timeline involves determining the project's timeline, including its start and end dates, as well as any key milestones along the way. This timeline helps to ensure that the project is completed within the specified timeframe.

6.6.7 Develop the overall project plan

The final step in creating a feasibility study is to develop a project plan that outlines the project's scope, timeline, budget, and resources. This plan helps to ensure that the project is properly planned and executed and that all stakeholders are aware of their roles and responsibilities.

Overall, creating a feasibility study involves assessing the project's viability from various perspectives, including market, technical, financial, and risk analyses. By following this process, project managers can determine whether a project is worth pursuing – or not - and can develop a solid plan to ensure its success if it is found to be viable.

6.6.8 The Sales Conference - Feasibility Study

The sales conference is a done deal in terms of feasibility because it's an annual event that needs to happen and is expected in the normal annual cycle for the company.

However, some aspects of the feasibility study should definitely be undertaken early such as initial risk planning, particularly around external factors that you may have less control over than some of the other stuff.

For instance, confirming external speakers and their availability on the dates required and setting up alternatives should your first choices either not be available or become unavailable during the planning process.

Another risk is that the hotel doesn't have enough accommodation for the requirements so confirming and pre-booking enough accommodation for all the sales staff partners, other company staff and external speakers will ensure that everybody is on site and taken care of.

Leaving this stuff until the last minute almost guarantees project failure, so early planning and booking of resources makes for much happier projects!

6.7 Developing the business case

Developing a strong business case is a crucial part of the project initiation process because it helps decision makers, stakeholders, and the public make well-informed, transparent choices. A business case serves as a management tool that not only outlines the rationale behind a specific policy, strategy, or project, but also establishes a framework for its delivery and performance monitoring.

6.7.1 Steps to create a business case

The process of developing a business case typically involves the following steps:

1. **Identifying the need for the project**: This step involves understanding the problem or opportunity that the project aims to address. This can include conducting a needs analysis, assessing the current situation, and identifying the stakeholders involved.

2. **Defining the objectives and scope of the project**: This step involves setting clear objectives and defining the scope of the project. This can include outlining the project's deliverables, timelines, budget, and resources required.

3. **Conducting a feasibility study**: This step involves assessing the feasibility of the project. This can include conducting a risk analysis, assessing the technical, economic, and environmental feasibility of the project, and identifying any potential constraints.

4. **Developing options and evaluating alternatives**: This step involves developing a range of options for addressing the problem or opportunity identified in step one. This can include evaluating the costs, benefits, and risks of each option and selecting the most viable option.

5. **Developing a business case**: This step involves documenting the results of the feasibility study and options analysis. This can include developing a comprehensive business case that outlines the project's benefits, costs, risks, and implementation plan.

6.7.2 Sample business case structure

Some of the major headings that should typically be included in a business case are:

1. **Executive summary**: A brief summary of the business case that provides an overview of the project's benefits, costs, and risks.

2. **Background**: A description of the problem or opportunity that the project aims to address.

3. **Objectives and scope**: A clear description of the project's objectives and scope.

4. **Feasibility study**: An assessment of the technical, economic, and environmental feasibility of the project.

5. **Options and alternatives**: A description of the range of options developed for addressing the problem or opportunity identified in step one.

6. **Evaluation of alternatives**: A detailed evaluation of the costs, benefits, and risks of each option.

7. **Recommended option**: A clear recommendation of the most viable option.

8. **Implementation plan**: A comprehensive plan for implementing the recommended option.

6.7.3 Benefits of having a good business case

There are many good reasons fo taking the time to create a solid business case. A well crafted case:

1. **Justifies the investment**: A well-crafted business case articulates the problem or opportunity at hand, as well as the proposed solution, to demonstrate the need for investment in a specific project. It allows stakeholders to evaluate the potential return on investment and make informed decisions about whether to proceed.

2. **Aligns with strategic objectives**: A business case helps ensure that a project aligns with an organization's strategic goals and objectives. By clearly outlining the project's purpose and intended outcomes, stakeholders can evaluate whether the project contributes to their overall vision.

3. **Facilitates stakeholder buy-in**: A business case presents evidence-based reasoning for a project, which can help gain the support and commitment of key stakeholders. This can be crucial to the project's success, as stakeholder buy-in is often necessary for securing resources and overcoming potential obstacles.

4. **Enables transparent decision-making**: A business case allows decision-makers to weigh the pros and cons of different options in a structured, transparent manner. This can lead to better decision-making and increased accountability.

5. **Provides a performance monitoring framework**: A business case outlines the project's objectives, key performance indicators (KPIs), and success criteria, which can be used to monitor progress and evaluate the project's overall performance. By establishing clear metrics, the business case serves as a reference point for stakeholders to track the project's outcomes and make necessary adjustments if it deviates from the initial plan.

6. **Identifies risks and mitigation strategies**: A comprehensive business case identifies potential risks associated with the project and proposes mitigation strategies. This proactive approach to risk management helps stakeholders anticipate and address challenges, reducing the likelihood of project delays or failures.

7. **Streamlines project planning**: A strong business case lays the foundation for project planning by outlining the project's scope, timelines, and required resources. This information can be used to develop a detailed project plan, ensuring that all parties have a clear understanding of their roles and responsibilities.

6.8 Project Charter

Creating a project charter is a critical step in project management as it helps to establish the project's objectives, goals, and scope. Here is an outline of the process of creating a project charter, including the key elements required within such a document:

1. **Define the project scope**: The first step in creating a project charter is to define the project's scope, including its objectives, deliverables, and key stakeholders. This helps to establish the project's overall purpose and what it aims to achieve.

2. **Identify the project sponsor**: The project sponsor is the person or group that is responsible for initiating and supporting the project. Identifying the project sponsor helps to ensure that there is a clear chain of command and accountability for the project.

3. **Define the project team**: The project team is the group of individuals who are responsible for executing the project. Defining the project team helps to ensure that there is a clear understanding of who is involved in the project and what their roles and responsibilities are.

4. **Develop the project timeline**: The project timeline outlines the project's start and end dates, as well as any key milestones and deadlines. Developing the project timeline helps to ensure that the project is completed within the specified timeframe.

5. **Establish the project budget**: The project budget outlines the project's financial requirements, including its costs, revenue, and profitability. Establishing the project budget helps to ensure that the project is financially viable and that resources are allocated appropriately.

6. **Identify potential risks**: Identifying potential risks involves assessing the project's risks, including potential issues that could impact the

project's success. This helps to develop strategies to mitigate potential risks and to ensure that the project is completed successfully.

7. **Define the project management approach**: The project management approach outlines the methodology and tools that will be used to manage the project. This helps to ensure that there is a clear plan for managing the project and that all team members are aware of how the project will be executed.

8. **Define the project deliverables**: The project deliverables are the tangible results that will be delivered by the project. Defining the project deliverables helps to ensure that there is a clear understanding of what the project aims to achieve and what outcomes are expected.

Overall, creating a project charter involves defining the project's scope, establishing the project team and sponsor, developing the project timeline and budget, identifying potential risks, defining the project management approach, and defining the project deliverables. By following this process, project managers can ensure that there is a clear plan for executing the project and that all stakeholders are aware of their roles and responsibilities.

6.8.1 The Sales Conference – Project Charter

Using the headings above, why not try creating a simple charter document to outline the answers to the different headings in relation to the sales conference case study. This will give you a good idea of what project charter document looks like and once you've got that information together, you should see that it brings together all the key points that everybody needs to know early on in the project planning process to ensure everyone is on the same page and aiming in the same direction.

6.9 Sustainability

Sustainability is an increasingly important concept for project managers to incorporate into early stage planning of any project. Stakeholders, be they customers and users or other interested parties are increasingly conscious of, and make decisions based on, sustainability concerns. So this is a key area of interest and action that project managers on projects of all sizes need to incorporate into project planning and execution from an early stage.

Here is an outline of how sustainability is important and how project managers can incorporate it into their early stage planning:

1. **Define sustainability:** The first step in incorporating sustainability into early stage project planning is to define what sustainability means in the context of the project. This involves considering the project's impact on the environment, society, and the economy.

2. **Conduct a sustainability analysis:** The sustainability analysis involves assessing the project's potential impact on the environment, society, and the economy. This analysis helps to identify potential sustainability issues and to develop strategies to mitigate them.

3. **Set sustainability goals:** Setting sustainability goals involves establishing measurable targets for the project's environmental, social, and economic impact. These goals can include reducing waste, conserving energy, improving social outcomes, and enhancing economic viability.

4. **Integrate sustainability into the project plan:** Integrating sustainability into the project plan involves considering sustainability factors at every stage of the project's lifecycle. This includes selecting sustainable materials, designing sustainable processes, and ensuring that the project is socially responsible.

5. **Engage stakeholders in sustainability planning:** Engaging stakeholders in sustainability planning involves communicating with all stakeholders about the project's sustainability goals and ensuring that they are aware of their role in achieving these goals. This can help to build support for the project and ensure that sustainability is considered throughout the project's lifecycle.

6. **Monitor and evaluate sustainability performance**: Monitoring and evaluating sustainability performance involves measuring the project's environmental, social, and economic impact and comparing it to the established sustainability goals. This helps to ensure that the project is on track and that sustainability is being considered throughout the project's lifecycle.

Overall, incorporating sustainability into early stage project planning involves defining sustainability, conducting a sustainability analysis, setting sustainability goals, integrating sustainability into the project plan, engaging stakeholders in sustainability planning, and monitoring and evaluating sustainability performance. By considering sustainability at every stage of the project's lifecycle, project managers can ensure that the project is environmentally, socially, and economically responsible and sustainable.

6.9.1   The Sales Conference - Sustainability

Sustainability is increasingly becoming a button topic for many people as well as companies. It's very easy to ignore or overlook sustainability when planning projects, but this is precisely the time when sustainability should be factored in. Early decisions around projects can dramatically affect the sustainability of how the project is run executed and the load that the project puts on the environment.

Do you really need everybody in the same hotel for a week? Co-located conferences are definitely fun, but they carry a huge burden in terms of travel, accommodation and use of resources that might otherwise be avoidable whilst still gaining sufficient business benefit.

And many conferences have swag bags and handouts for guests, and these can often be sourced quite cheaply, but are such goods manufactured sustainably? Are the supply chains for such goods ones that your company would want to stand over and be associated with? Could you source more environmentally friendly goods, or perhaps even decide not to hand out stuff which many people may not really want anyway, and instead donate funds to some good cause, charity or non-profit?

There's no definitive right answer here, but these are questions that should be asked in the early stages of planning.

6.10 Ethics

Project management is a complex task that involves planning, organizing, and executing projects to achieve specific goals. However, it's important to note that the success of a project isn't just measured by its outcomes, but also by how it's conducted. That's why building ethical considerations into project planning and execution is essential.

Ethics refer to a set of moral principles that govern the behaviour of individuals or organizations. In project management, ethical considerations are important because they guide the behaviour of project managers and team members, ensuring that the project is conducted in a responsible and transparent manner.

One of the primary reasons why ethics is essential in project management is that it helps to ensure that the project is conducted with integrity. Ethical behaviour ensures that all stakeholders are treated fairly and with respect, that the project is executed transparently, and that conflicts of interest are avoided.

Building ethical considerations into project planning and execution can also help to prevent legal issues and reputational damage. By conducting the project in an ethical manner, project managers can avoid violating laws and regulations, which could lead to legal action against the organization. Moreover, by prioritizing ethical behaviour, the organization can build a positive reputation, which can lead to increased trust from customers, partners, and other stakeholders.

Finally, ethical considerations can also help to ensure that the project is conducted sustainably. By taking into account the impact of the project on the environment, society, and future generations, project managers can ensure that the project's benefits outweigh its negative consequences.

6.10.1 The Sales Conference - Ethics

Linked with sustainability, ethical practices by companies are now increasingly shining a spotlight on decision made and whether or not they "should" be made.

Is it really ethical to spend so much money on flying people in from all over the world, using hotels, taxis and the like when much of the work could be done remotely via Zoom or Teams?

On the other hand, co-location builds esprit-de-corps – fosters relationship building and can facilitate networking that can have positive consequences long after the physical meetings have concluded. The key thing here is to factor these types of questions into the decision making process so they are made for the right reasons, and not just becuase it's the way it's always been done.

7 Project Planning

Once we've kicked the tires on the idea of the project and got a general go ahead to proceed, we move into project planning.

This is probably the most important part of the project and one which people unfamiliar with project management very often think can be skipped over or short-cutted. Nothing could be further from the truth. Planning a project should take anything up to 50% of the elapsed time that you have to do the project. Why? Because laying out a plan allows you to look down the road between where you are now and where you need to be, and put things in place to enable effective and safe travel down the planned pathway.

With 70 odd years of formal project management and discipline now in place, it's clear from much research, both empirical and academic, that time spent planning is time well spent.

If things go wrong in a project - and they always do - the finger will definitely point back at you and hard questions will be asked if you can't show at least a degree of formalised planning.

In preparing for battle I have always found that plans are useless but planning is indispensable.

Dwight D. Eisenhower

So let's have a look through this stage of the process and break it down into its constituent elements...

7.1 Applying ECCSR to the planning phase

In the project planning process, it's essential for a project manager to incorporate sustainability and ethics to ensure that the project aligns with both environmental and social responsibilities. Here are some practical examples of how a project manager can build in these concepts:

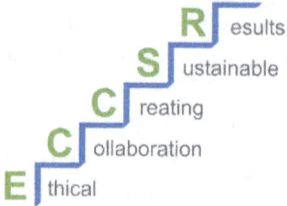

1. **Identify sustainable objectives**: When defining project goals, include specific sustainability targets, such as reducing energy consumption, minimising waste, or using eco-friendly materials. These objectives should align with the company's overall sustainability strategy and follow relevant regulations and guidelines.

2. **Stakeholder engagement**: Engage with all stakeholders, including employees, suppliers, customers, and local communities, to understand their expectations and concerns. This will allow you to identify potential ethical issues and incorporate their feedback into the project scope, helping to create a more inclusive and responsible project.

3. **Ethical supply chain management**: When selecting suppliers, consider their environmental and social performance alongside cost and quality. Evaluate their adherence to ethical labour practices, environmental regulations, and fair trade standards. Building these criteria into your procurement process will promote responsible sourcing and strengthen your project's ethical foundations.

4. **Life-cycle assessment**: Consider the environmental impact of the project throughout its entire life cycle, from the initial planning stages to its end-of-life disposal.

5. **Sustainable design principles**: Integrate sustainable design principles such as energy efficiency, water conservation, and waste reduction into the project design. This can help minimise the environmental footprint and reduce long-term operational costs.

6. **Training and education**: Educate team members about the importance of sustainability and ethical practices, and provide them with the necessary training to implement these principles. This will empower them to make informed decisions throughout the project's lifecycle, ensuring that sustainability and ethics remain at the forefront.

7. **Monitor and measure**: Establish key performance indicators (KPIs) to track your project's progress towards its sustainability and ethical objectives. Regularly monitor and report on these KPIs to stakeholders, using the results to make adjustments and improvements where necessary.

8. **Transparent communication**: Communicate openly and honestly about the project's sustainability and ethical performance to stakeholders, both internally and externally. Transparency is key to building trust and demonstrating commitment to responsible project management.

9. **Encourage innovation**: Foster a culture of innovation and creativity within the project team, encouraging team members to come up with new ideas and solutions that promote sustainability and ethical practices. This can lead to the discovery of more efficient and environmentally friendly methods, ultimately improving the project's overall performance.

10. **Continuous improvement**: After the project's completion, conduct a thorough review of its sustainability and ethical performance. Use the lessons learned to inform future projects, continuously enhancing your project management practices in these areas.

7.1.1 The Global Reporting Initiative (GRI)

This independent international organisation develops sustainability reporting standards to help businesses, governments, and other organisations measure and communicate their economic, environmental, and social impacts. When planning a project, a project manager can use GRI's framework to build in sustainable approachs and measures, and share the results with stakeholders. This transparency and communication can lead to better ethical collaboration and sustainable results in future projects.

The GRI Initiative website is at https://www.globalreporting.org/

By incorporating these steps into the project planning and scoping process, a project manager can effectively build sustainability and ethics into the core of the project. This not only benefits the environment and society but also contributes to the long-term success and reputation of the business.

7.2 Creating a Project Plan

Creating a project plan is an important step for any project manager. It helps to ensure that everyone involved in the project understands their roles and responsibilities, the project objectives, timelines, and budgets. Here are the steps required to create a generic project plan:

1. **Define project objectives** - The first step in creating a project plan is to define the project objectives. This involves identifying the project's purpose, goals, and desired outcomes. It's important to ensure that the objectives are clear, specific, and measurable.

2. **Identify project stakeholders** - Next, identify the stakeholders involved in the project. This includes project sponsors, team members, and other stakeholders who may be affected by the project's outcomes. It's important to communicate with stakeholders throughout the project to ensure their support and involvement.

3. **Develop project scope** - The project scope defines the boundaries of the project. It outlines what is and isn't included in the project and identifies any constraints that may impact the project's outcomes. A well-defined project scope is essential for ensuring that the project stays on track and within budget.

4. **Create a work breakdown structure** (WBS) - The WBS breaks down the project into smaller, more manageable components. This helps to identify specific tasks that need to be completed to achieve project objectives. The WBS should include all project deliverables and be organized in a hierarchical structure.

5. **Develop project timelines** - The project timeline outlines the start and end dates for each task in the WBS. It also identifies any dependencies between tasks and provides a roadmap for the project. Developing a realistic timeline is important for ensuring

that the project is completed on time. The Gantt chart is a great way to visualize a project – see page 113.

6. **Determine resource requirements** - Identify the resources required to complete the project. This includes personnel, equipment, and materials. It's important to ensure that the resources are available when needed and that they are allocated efficiently.

7. **Identify potential risks** - Identify potential risks that could impact the project's outcomes. This includes external risks such as market changes or regulatory requirements, as well as internal risks such as delays or resource constraints. Develop a risk management plan to mitigate and manage these risks.

8. **Develop a budget** - Develop a budget that outlines the project's costs, including personnel, equipment, and materials. Ensure that the budget is realistic and takes into account all costs associated with the project.

9. **Establish project communication plan** - Develop a communication plan that outlines how project information will be shared with stakeholders. This includes the frequency of communication, the channels to be used, and the format of the information.

10. **Monitor and control project progress** - Monitor project progress against the timeline and budget. This involves tracking project milestones, identifying any deviations from the plan, and taking corrective action if necessary.

In conclusion, creating a project plan involves defining project objectives, identifying project stakeholders, developing project scope, creating a work breakdown structure, developing project timelines, determining resource requirements, identifying potential risks, developing a budget, establishing a project communication plan, and monitoring and controlling project progress.

By following these steps, project managers can raise the chances that their projects are completed on time, within budget, and to the satisfaction of stakeholders.

7.3 Work Breakdown Structure – What needs to be done

A Work Breakdown Structure (WBS) is a project management tool used to break down a large project into smaller, more manageable components or tasks. IWBS is typically represented as a hierarchical diagram with different levels of boxes representing tasks, sub-tasks and sub-sub-tasks down to however many levels of detail are required. This will depend on the complexity of the project.

The term "work breakdown structure" originated from the aerospace industry in the 1950s, where it was used to organize complex projects like building airplanes. It's a really useful tool to help you as the project manager and your team visualise all the different tasks that are required in order to make the project actually happen.

To create a work breakdown structure for a project, follow these steps:

1. Define the project scope: Clearly define the project objectives and what is included in the project.

2. Identify the major deliverables: Break down the project into major deliverables or components. These should be the highest level of detail in the WBS.

3. Break down the major deliverables: Break down the major deliverables into smaller, more manageable components or tasks.

4. Organize the work: Organize the tasks or components into a hierarchical structure. This structure should show how the components are related to one another and how they contribute to the project as a whole.

5. Assign codes to the components: Assign codes to the components to make them easier to identify and manage.

6. Validate the WBS: Review the WBS to ensure that all tasks are included and that there are no duplications or omissions. This is best done with the team so that differing levels of expertise and experience can inform the task list that is being set up for the project. It's also a great way to get everybody on the same page in terms of what is going to have to be done.

7. Use the WBS to create a project schedule: Use the WBS to create a project schedule by estimating the duration of each task or component and determining their dependencies.

Creating a work breakdown structure is a critical step in project management, as it helps to ensure that all project components are identified, managed, and executed effectively.

7.3.1 WBS Tools

Creating work breakdown structure diagrams is typically done with a diagramming tool that allows you to create hierarchical levels of boxes connected by lines. There are a number of such tools available on the market, some of which are outlined below. MS Word Outline View

An easy way of generating work breakdown structure is, although in a slightly non-standard format, is to use the outline view in MS Word. This effectively turns the work breakdown structure on its side and allows you to create an indented, hierarchical view of whatever list of tasks you are creating.

The screenshot here shows a simple house build example and using this tool which almost everybody has at their disposal, even if they didn't know it existed!

I use the outline view a lot, because it's very easy to brainstorm and unstructured list and then quickly organise it into a hierarchy.
You can indent points using the Tab key, the single arrows either side of the level drop down at the top of the screen, or even using drag and drop. You can outdent using Shift+Tab, the arrows or drag and drop.

An online tutorial on how to use the Word Outline view can be found at https://www.dummies.com/article/technology/software/microsoft-products/word/how-writers-can-use-word-2019s-outline-view-259128/

Project Management made easy...

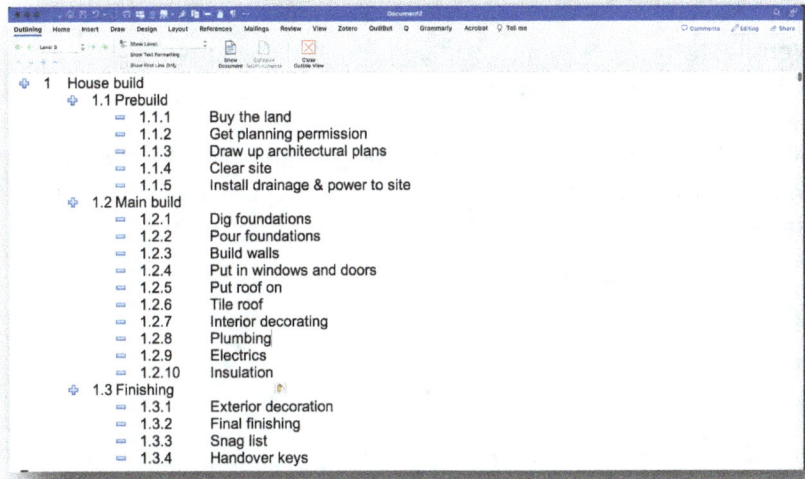

7.3.1.1 Microsoft Visio

Website: https://www.microsoft.com/en-ie/microsoft-365/visio/flowchart-software

Microsoft Visio has for many years, been the go to tool for diagramming and it's still an excellent way to generate work breakdown structure diagrams.

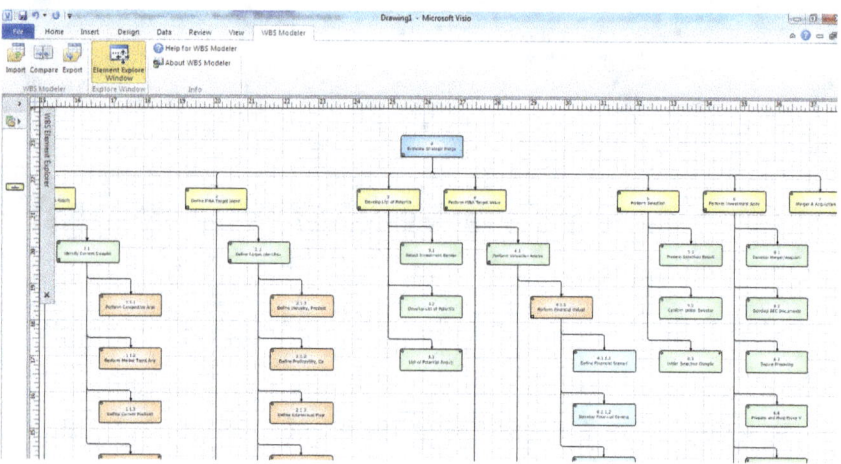

Project Management made easy...

7.3.1.2 LucidChart

Website: https://www.lucidchart.com/

Lucid chart is a good alternative to Visio which has a free tier, making it useful as a an occasional diagramming tool, without needing to invest money on buying or subscribing.

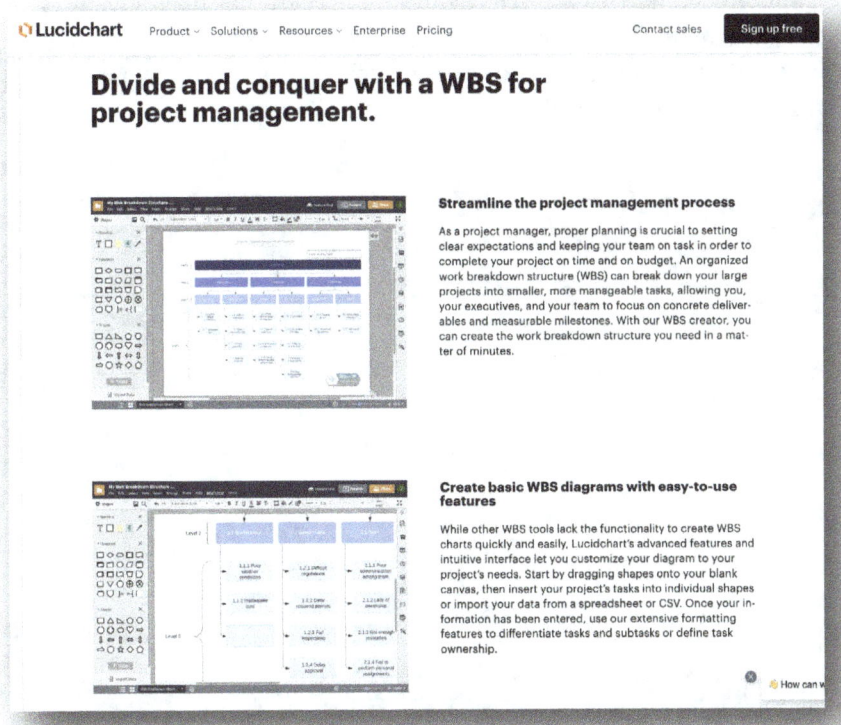

Project Management made easy…

7.3.1.3   MS Powerpoint

And then of course there is MS PowerPoint. Hidden away in the menu structure is a tool to create work breakdown structure is simply and easily. It's not suitable for complex WBS diagrams, but for those with just three or four levels and not too many boxes, it's an easy and accessible way to generate this type of visualisation.

To generate a SmartArt WBS, navigate to the Hierarchy diagrams by clicking on the Insert option on the top menu, then choosing SmartArt from the ribbon and finally click on Hierarchy in the drop-down list. Choose your preferred style of diagram and off you go!

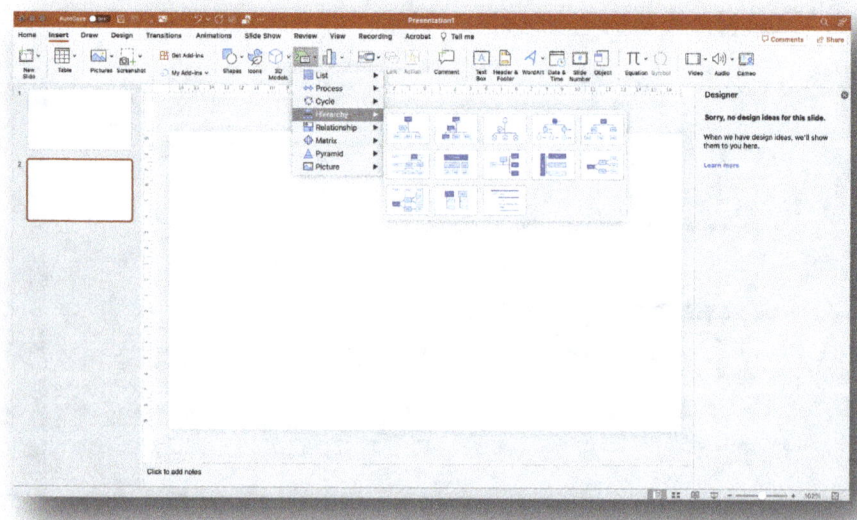

Project Management made easy...

7.3.2 The Sales Conference - WBS

Here's how a basic WBS might look like done using PowerPoint:

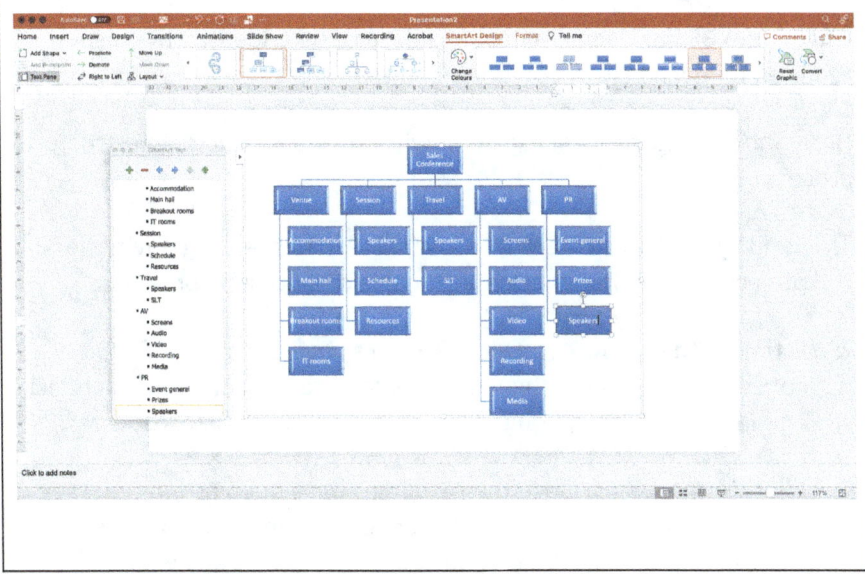

7.4 Resource Planning

Following on from the creation of a task list for your project, which is done with the work breakdown structure tool, you now need to figure out what resources your project requires in order to complete those tasks.

Once the WBS has been created, it is necessary to identify the resources required for each task or component in the project.

Here's how resource planning fits in with the work breakdown structure process:

1. **Identify the tasks:** The WBS process involves breaking down the project into smaller, more manageable components or tasks.

2. **Estimate the resources:** Once the tasks have been identified, it is necessary to estimate the resources required to complete each task. This includes people, equipment, materials, and other resources.

3. **Allocate resources:** Once the resources have been estimated, they need to be allocated to each task or component. This involves determining who will be responsible for each task and what resources they will need to complete it.

4. **Create a resource schedule:** After the resources have been allocated, a resource schedule can be created. This schedule outlines when each resource will be needed and for how long.

5. **Monitor resource usage:** During the project, it is important to monitor the usage of resources to ensure that they are being used effectively and efficiently. This involves tracking how much time and money is being spent on each resource and making adjustments as necessary.

Effective resource planning can help to ensure that a project is completed on time and within budget. By identifying the resources required for each task or component, it is possible to allocate resources effectively and ensure that they are being used efficiently throughout the project. This can help to minimize the risk of delays and cost overruns, and ultimately increase the chances of project success.

7.5 Risk Management Planning

Risk management is an important aspect of project management that involves identifying, assessing, and mitigating potential risks that may impact a project.

Effective risk management and planning can help to ensure that a project is completed on time, within budget, and to the desired quality. Here's why risk management is important and how to conduct an effective risk management analysis for a project:

Risk Management helps:

1. **Identify potential risks:** Risk management helps to identify potential risks that could impact a project, allowing the project team to plan and prepare for them in advance.

2. **Mitigate risks:** By identifying potential risks, the project team can take steps to mitigate them and reduce their impact on the project.

3. **Reduce uncertainty:** Risk management can help to reduce uncertainty and increase the chances of project success by identifying potential risks and developing contingency plans to address them.

4. **Manage costs:** Effective risk management can help to manage project costs by identifying potential risks that could impact the project budget and taking steps to mitigate them.

7.5.1 Steps for Conducting an Effective Risk Management Analysis

The outputs from a risk analysis will typically be gathered together in a document known as a risk register. This will list all the risks and then categorise them, as well as showing appropriate responses or mitigating actions that should be taken in order to address the risk.

The risk register should be seen as a living document that is updated on a regular basis, because risks can change due to circumstances evolving throughout the life of the project.

Describing risks is a key first step, and doing this well can really make a difference to the effectiveness of your risk planning. I like to define a risk as a **potential negative consequence event.**

If you use this definition when thinking about risk, it encourages you to define risks as events that you want to avoid happening as opposed to more generalised issue areas that are far more difficult to plan against.

7.5.2   The Risk recipe

Another good way to clarify risks when first describing them is to **use the recipe <risk event> <effect> <cause>.**

An example might be "There's a risk that <the stage projector will fail> causing <our presenter to not be able to complete their presentation> leading to <our sales teams not learning about Strategic Selling>"

Having explained the risk in this way, the focus on mitigating, the risk of the stage projector failing might be to have a second projector on hand, a spare bulb for the projector, or perhaps a large screen that could be used instead of the projected image. All of these are valid and viable mitigations to put in place for a risk of this sort, but they are far easier to get to once the risk has been described in this way.

7.5.3   Identify potential risks

The first step in risk management is to identify potential risks that could impact the project. This can be done through brainstorming sessions, historical data analysis, and other techniques, such as the PESTEL & SWOT tools.

Project Management made easy...

7.5.4 PESTEL

The PESTEL tool is a framework used in business analysis to identify and evaluate the external factors that may impact an organization or project. The tool stands for:

P - Political E - Economic S - Social T - Technological E - Environmental L - Legal

The PESTEL tool originated as a strategic management tool in the 1960s and 1970s, and is commonly used today in project management risk analysis to identify potential external risks that may impact a project.

Here's a brief description of how the PESTEL tool might be applied in project management risk analysis:

a. **Political**: This factor looks at the impact of government policy and regulations on the project. For example, changes in tax laws or new regulations could impact the project's timeline or budget.

b. **Economic**: This factor looks at the economic conditions that may impact the project, such as inflation or changes in interest rates. These factors may impact the availability of resources or the project budget.

c. **Social**: This factor looks at the impact of social trends and changes on the project, such as changes in consumer behavior or demographics. For example, a project that targets an aging population may need to consider the impact of an aging workforce.

d. **Technological**: This factor looks at the impact of technological developments on the project, such as changes in software or hardware that may impact project timelines or costs.

e. **Environmental**: This factor looks at the impact of environmental factors on the project, such as changes in weather patterns or environmental regulations. For example, a project that involves construction in a flood-prone area may need to consider the potential impact of flooding on the project timeline and budget.

f. **Legal**: This factor looks at the impact of legal factors on the project, such as changes in laws or regulations that may impact the project timeline or budget. For example, changes in data protection laws may require additional resources to be allocated to ensure compliance.

By using the PESTEL tool in project management risk analysis, project managers can identify and evaluate external factors that may impact the project, and develop strategies to mitigate those risks. This can help to ensure that the project is completed on time, within budget, and to the desired quality.

7.5.5 The SWOT tool

The SWOT tool is another useful focussing tool for Risk Analysis. It's a commonly used framework in business analysis and project management, and is an acronym for:

S - Strengths W - Weaknesses O - Opportunities T - Threats

The SWOT tool was developed in the 1960s by Albert Humphrey, a management consultant who led a research project at Stanford University. It has since become a widely used tool in business and project management.

Here's how each letter can be applied in project management risk analysis:

Strengths: This factor looks at the internal strengths of the project or organization, such as the skills and expertise of the project team, the project's financial resources, or the organization's reputation. By identifying strengths, project managers can leverage them to mitigate risks and improve project outcomes.

Weaknesses: This factor looks at the internal weaknesses of the project or organization, such as gaps in the team's skills or experience, limited financial resources, or poor project management processes. By identifying weaknesses, project managers can take steps to address them and reduce the impact they may have on the project.

Opportunities: This factor looks at the external opportunities that may impact the project, such as new markets, emerging technologies, or changes in consumer behaviour. By identifying opportunities, project managers can adjust the project plan to take advantage of these trends and reduce potential risks.

Threats: This factor looks at the external threats that may impact the project, such as changes in regulations, economic downturns, or increased competition. By identifying threats, project managers can develop contingency plans to mitigate their impact and reduce the risk of project failure.

By using the SWOT tool in project management risk analysis, project managers can identify and evaluate internal and external factors that may impact the project, and develop strategies to mitigate risks and take advantage of opportunities. This can help to ensure that the project is completed on time, within budget, and to the desired quality.

7.5.6 Assess the likelihood and impact of each risk

Once potential risks have been identified, the likelihood and impact of each risk should be assessed. This involves evaluating the probability of the risk occurring and the potential impact it could have on the project.

Likelihood and impact are typically plotted on a grid known as a risk matrix, that is either 5 by 5 or 10 x 10. The risks that score highest cluster in the top right hand corner of such a risk matrix and are typically the ones that will be worked on first and allocated resources to address the risks concerned.

7.5.7 Develop risk mitigation strategies

After assessing the risks, the project team should develop risk mitigation strategies to reduce the likelihood or impact of each risk. This may involve developing contingency plans, identifying alternative approaches, or implementing risk-reducing measures.

Risk mitigation strategies are actions that are taken to reduce the likelihood or impact of potential risks on a project. These strategies are an important part of project management, as they help to minimize the impact of risks and increase the chances of project success. Here are some common risk mitigation strategies:

a. **Avoidance**: This strategy involves avoiding or eliminating the risk altogether. For example, if a project involves a high degree of risk, a project manager may decide to abandon the project altogether rather than proceed with it.

b. **Transference**: This strategy involves transferring the risk to a third party. For example, a project manager may purchase insurance to transfer the risk of loss or damage to the project.

c. **Acceptance**: This strategy involves accepting the risk and taking steps to minimize its impact. For example, a project manager may allocate additional resources to address the risk or develop contingency plans to mitigate its impact.

d. **Reduction**: This strategy involves taking steps to reduce the likelihood or impact of the risk. For example, a project manager may implement additional quality control measures to reduce the risk of defects or errors.

e. **Contingency Planning**: This strategy involves developing a plan to address the risk if it occurs. For example, a project manager may develop a contingency plan to address potential delays or cost overruns.

f. **Mitigation Planning**: This strategy involves developing a plan to reduce the impact of the risk if it occurs. For example, a project manager may develop a mitigation plan to minimize the impact of a potential data breach.

7.5.8   Implement risk mitigation strategies

Once risk mitigation strategies have been developed, they should be implemented as part of the project plan. This may involve adjusting project timelines, allocating additional resources, or making other changes to the project plan.

7.5.9   Monitor and review risks

Throughout the project, risks should be monitored and reviewed to ensure that risk mitigation strategies are effective and that new risks are identified and addressed in a timely manner.

By following these steps, project managers can conduct an effective risk management analysis that helps to reduce uncertainty, manage costs, and increase the chances of project success.

7.5.10   The Sales Conference - Risks

Lots can go wrong when planning any event!

Speakers may not show, or be delayed, equipment and lighting can fail, the venue double books and only lets you know the day before – one of my student teams planning an event some years ago had their venue burn down the day before the event!

So having Plan B's for as many risks as possible are really important, especially in a scenario such as this, where mistakes are very public.

7.6 Some risk examples in business projects

One well-known tech company that has implemented risk management concepts in project management is Google. For example, when Google began work on its self-driving car project, the company recognized the inherent risks involved in developing such a revolutionary technology. To manage these risks, the company implemented a rigorous testing process, including simulation testing, to ensure that the technology was safe and effective.

Google also utilized risk management techniques during the development of its Google Glass technology. The company identified potential risks associated with the technology, such as privacy concerns and issues with the design, and implemented strategies to mitigate these risks.

Effective communication also played a crucial role in managing risks during both of these projects. Google project managers ensured that team members were communicating effectively, sharing information about potential risks and working collaboratively to address these risks.

7.7 Project Schedule – When will tasks be done?

A project schedule is a document that outlines the tasks and activities required to complete a project, including their start and end dates, dependencies, and resources required. The project schedule is a critical component of project management, as it helps to ensure that the project is completed on time and within budget.

The concept of project scheduling originated in the field of construction management in the early 20th century, and has since become a widely used tool in project management across a variety of industries.

Here are the practical steps a project manager can follow to create a project schedule:

1. **Identify the project tasks:** The first step in creating a project schedule is to identify all of the tasks and activities required to complete the project. This can be done through brainstorming sessions, work breakdown structure analysis, or other techniques.

2. **Define the task dependencies:** Once the tasks have been identified, it is necessary to define the dependencies between them. This involves determining which tasks need to be completed before others can start.

3. **Estimate the task durations:** Once the task dependencies have been defined, the next step is to estimate the duration of each task. This can be done using historical data, expert judgment, or other methods.

4. **Allocate resources:** After the task durations have been estimated, resources need to be allocated to each task. This involves determining who will be responsible for each task and what resources they will need to complete it.

5. **Develop the project schedule:** Once the tasks have been defined, dependencies have been determined, and resources allocated, a project schedule can be developed. The project schedule should include start and end dates for each task, as well as the critical path, which is the sequence of tasks that must be completed on time for the project to be completed on schedule.

6. **Monitor the project schedule:** Throughout the project, it is important to monitor the project schedule to ensure that tasks are being completed on time and that the project is on track. If delays or other issues arise, the project schedule may need to be adjusted to ensure that the project is completed on time and within budget.

By following these steps, project managers can create an effective project schedule that helps to ensure that the project is completed on time and within budget. The project schedule is a critical tool in project management, and should be updated regularly to reflect changes in project scope, resource availability, or other factors that may impact the project timeline.

7.7.1 The Gantt chart

One of THE most useful communication tools in project management, the Gantt chart is a type of bar chart that illustrates a project schedule and the dependencies between project tasks. It was developed by Henry Gantt in the early 1900s, and has since become a widely used tool in project management.

A Gantt chart typically shows the start and end dates of each task or activity in a project, as well as their duration and any dependencies between them. This allows project managers to visualise the project schedule and identify critical paths, which are the sequences of tasks that must be completed on time for the project to be completed on schedule.

Gantt charts are used in project management to manage projects effectively in several ways:

1. **Visualize the project schedule:** Gantt charts allow project managers to visualize the project schedule and identify any potential issues, such as tasks that are behind schedule or dependencies that have not been properly identified.

2. **Track progress:** Gantt charts can be used to track the progress of each task or activity in a project, allowing project managers to monitor the project schedule and make adjustments as necessary.

3. **Allocate resources:** Gantt charts can help project managers to allocate resources effectively by showing which tasks or activities require the most resources and when they will be needed.

4. **Communicate with stakeholders:** Gantt charts can be used to communicate the project schedule and progress to stakeholders, including team members, sponsors, and customers.

5. **Identify critical paths**: Gantt charts can help project managers to identify critical paths, which are the sequences of tasks that must be completed on time for the project to be completed on schedule. By identifying critical paths, project managers can focus their attention and resources on those tasks to ensure that they are completed on time.

7.7.2 Recommended Gantt chart tools

Creating Gantt charts is a task that takes some time and patience. There are a number of excellent tools on the market that can make the process of creating and maintaining Gantt charts, relatively easy. Some of these are free to use and others require a subscription or payment.

7.7.2.1 Microsoft Excel – NO!

One tool that I do NOT recommend to create Gantt charts is Microsoft Excel. Although this is put forward by many as a way of creating Gantt charts easily, unless you are pretty skilled at programming, keeping an Excel Gantt chart updated as changes occur in the project is a tedious and very manual process. For this reason **I don't recommend using Excel – there are much better tools out there that make the job much easier**.

7.7.2.2 ClickUp

Website: https://clickup.com/

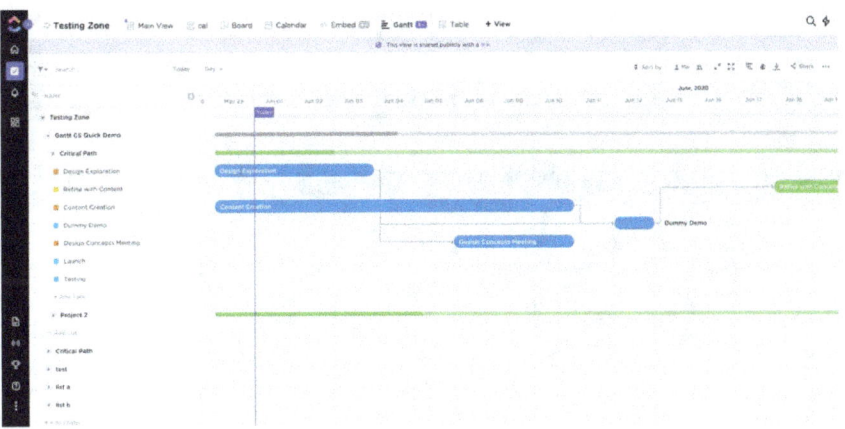

Project Management made easy...

7.7.2.3 TeamGantt

Website: https://www.teamgantt.com/

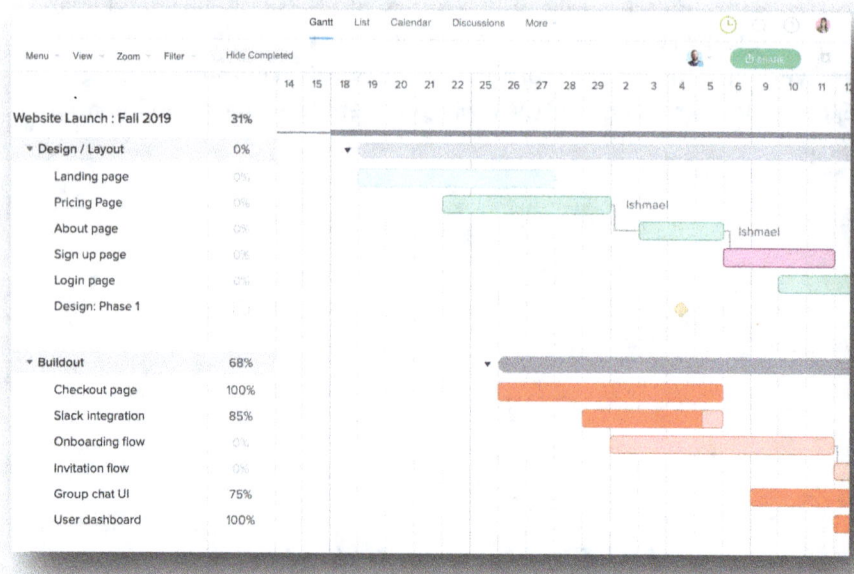

7.7.2.4 Microsoft Project

Website: https://www.microsoft.com/en-ie/microsoft-365/project/project-management-software

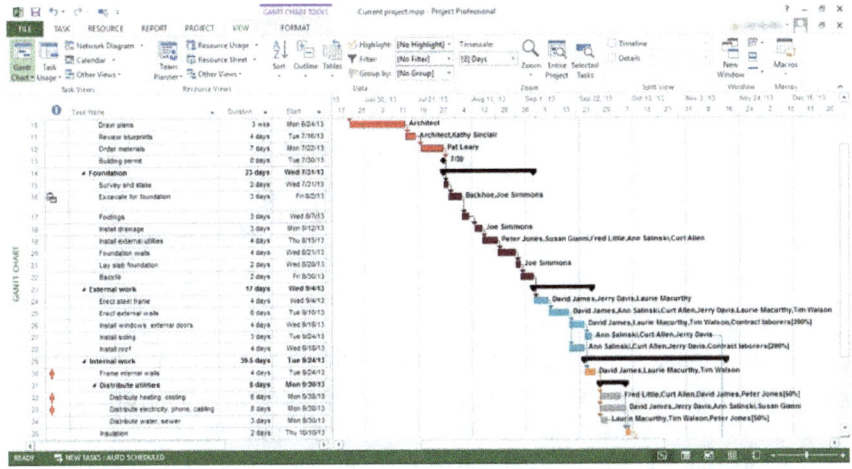

Project Management made easy...

7.7.2.5 Microsoft Planner

Website: https://tasks.office.com/

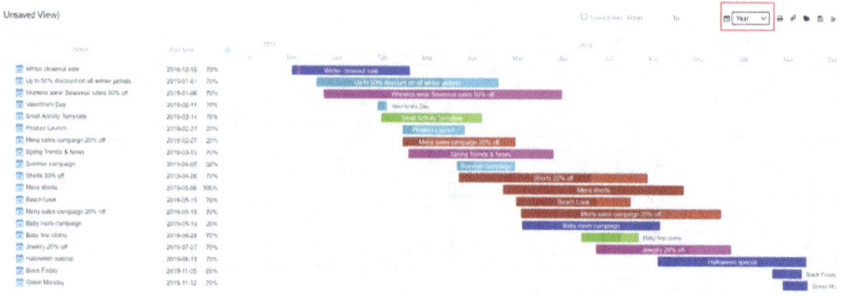

Overall, Gantt charts are a powerful tool in project management that can help project managers to manage projects effectively, monitor progress, and ensure that the project is completed on time and within budget. By visualizing the project schedule and identifying critical paths, project managers can make informed decisions and take timely action to ensure project success.

7.8 Finances – how much will this all cost?

Effective financial management is a critical component of successful project planning and execution. From the initial budgeting phase to ongoing monitoring and control, a strong understanding of the financial aspects of a project can help ensure its successful delivery and long-term viability.

Personally, throughout my project management career dealing with the finances around the project is one of my least favourite activities so this is definitely an area where I always brought somebody in who enjoys and is good at managing the money and tracking and reporting against it.

7.8.1   Budgeting and Estimating Costs

The foundation of financial management in project planning is the development of an accurate and comprehensive budget. This involves estimating the costs associated with various project activities, including:

a. **Labour**: Calculate the cost of salaries, wages, and benefits for project team members, as well as any external consultants or contractors.

b. **Materials and equipment**: Estimate the cost of purchasing, renting, or leasing the necessary materials and equipment for the project. Using the Work Breakdown Structure (WBS) – see page 94 - where all the separate tasks that make up the project are laid out can be a very useful way to make sure that all materials and equipment required have been identified, and relevant costs included in the estimates.

c. **Travel and logistics**: Account for expenses related to travel, accommodations, transportation, and other logistics.

d. **Licensing and permits**: Include the cost of obtaining any required licenses, permits, or regulatory approvals.

e. **Contingency**: Allocate a contingency fund to cover unexpected expenses or cost overruns.

f. **Overhead**: Factor in indirect costs such as office space, utilities, and administrative support.

7.8.2 Cash Flow Management

Cash flow management is crucial to ensuring the financial health of a project. Project managers should develop a cash flow forecast to anticipate the timing of expenses and revenues, allowing for effective allocation of financial resources throughout the project lifecycle.

Key elements of cash flow management include:

a. **Monitoring expenses**: Regularly track actual expenses against budgeted amounts to identify any discrepancies and make necessary adjustments.

b. **Invoicing and collections**: Ensure timely invoicing for completed project milestones and monitor collections to maintain a healthy cash flow.

c. **Payment scheduling**: Coordinate payment schedules with suppliers, contractors, and other stakeholders to optimize cash flow and maintain positive relationships.

d. **Financial reporting**: Provide regular financial reports to stakeholders, including updates on the project's cash flow status and any variances from the initial budget.

7.8.3 Financial Risk Management

Financial risks can significantly impact a project's success. Effective risk management involves identifying, analysing, and mitigating potential financial risks, such as:

a. **Cost overruns**: Establish contingency plans and closely monitor project activities to prevent unexpected costs from derailing the project.

b. **Currency fluctuations**: For international projects, consider implementing currency hedging strategies to minimize the impact of exchange rate fluctuations on project finances.

c. **Market conditions**: Stay informed about market trends and economic factors that could affect the project's financial viability, and adjust plans accordingly.

d. **Funding disruptions**: Develop alternative funding sources or contingency plans in case the project's primary funding source becomes unavailable.

7.8.4   Financial Performance Metrics

Tracking and analysing financial performance metrics can help project managers evaluate the project's financial health and make data-driven decisions. Key financial performance metrics include:

a. **Return on Investment (ROI):** Calculate the ROI by comparing the project's benefits to its costs, providing an indication of the project's overall financial success.

b. **Cost Variance (CV):** Assess the difference between the project's actual costs and the budgeted costs, offering insight into the project's financial performance.

c. **Schedule Variance (SV):** Measure the difference between the planned budget for work completed and the actual budget spent, which can indicate the project's efficiency in terms of time and resources.

d. **Cost Performance Index (CPI):** Calculate the ratio of earned value (the value of completed work) to actual costs, providing an indication of the project's cost efficiency.

e. **Budget at Completion (BAC):** Estimate the total budget required to complete the project, allowing for a comparison between planned and actual expenses as the project progresses.

7.8.5   Financial Controls and Governance

Establishing robust financial controls and governance processes helps maintain the financial integrity of the project and ensures compliance with relevant regulations and standards. Key elements of financial controls and governance include:

a. **Financial policies and procedures**: Develop clear, well-documented financial policies and procedures to guide team members and stakeholders in their financial decision-making and activities.

b. **Segregation of duties**: Implement appropriate segregation of duties to reduce the risk of fraud and errors, ensuring that no single individual has control over all aspects of a financial transaction.

c. **Regular audits and reviews**: Conduct periodic internal and external audits to assess the project's financial health, compliance, and the effectiveness of financial controls.

d. **Financial decision-making**: Establish a clear decision-making framework for financial matters, including the roles and responsibilities of project team members and stakeholders.

7.8.6   Financial Change Management

As projects evolve, changes in scope, timelines, and resources can have a significant impact on the project's financial health. Effective change management involves:

a. **Identifying potential changes**: Monitor project progress and proactively identify potential changes that could affect the project's finances.

b. **Evaluating the financial impact**: Assess the financial implications of proposed changes, including costs, benefits, and risks.

c. **Approving changes**: Develop a process for reviewing and approving change requests, ensuring that financial considerations are factored into decision-making.

d. **Updating financial plans**: Adjust budgets, cash flow forecasts, and financial performance metrics as necessary to reflect approved changes.

8 Project Execution

The execution phase is a pivotal stage in the project lifecycle, marking the transition from planning to action. This phase is crucial as it involves the actual implementation of the project plan, transforming concepts and strategies into tangible deliverables. During the execution phase, the project manager and team members work diligently to complete tasks, allocate resources, and monitor progress to ensure the project stays on track, adhering to the established timeline, budget, and quality standards. A successful execution phase lays the groundwork for the project's long-term success and its ability to meet stakeholder expectations.

Several key considerations should be taken into account when starting the execution phase of a project:

1. **Resource management**: Efficient allocation and management of resources, including personnel, equipment, and materials, are vital for smooth project execution. Project managers should ensure that resources are deployed effectively and according to the project plan.

2. **Communication:** Clear and consistent communication is essential to ensure all team members and stakeholders remain informed and engaged throughout the execution phase. Establishing effective communication channels and providing regular updates can help prevent misunderstandings and keep everyone aligned with project objectives.

3. **Task prioritization**: Prioritizing tasks based on their importance, urgency, and dependencies can help streamline the execution process. Project managers should continually reassess task priorities and make adjustments as necessary to keep the project on schedule.

4. **Quality control**: Implementing quality control measures is critical to ensure that project deliverables meet the required standards. Regular quality checks, reviews, and inspections can help identify potential issues and facilitate timely corrective actions.

5. **Risk management**: Continuously monitoring and addressing risks during the execution phase can help minimize potential disruptions and ensure the project stays on track. Proactively identifying, evaluating, and mitigating risks can safeguard the project's success.

8.1 Applying ECCSR to the Execution phase

During the project execution process, a project manager can integrate the concepts of ECCSR (ethical collaboration creating sustainable results) to ensure the project not only delivers its objectives but also upholds ethical and sustainable practices. Here are some practical examples of how to build ECCSR into the running, monitoring, and control of a project:

1. **Open communication channels**: Establish open and transparent communication channels within the team and with stakeholders. This encourages collaboration and helps to maintain an ethical working environment, addressing any potential issues before they escalate.

2. **Set clear expectations**: Clearly communicate expectations around ethical behaviour, sustainability, and collaboration within the project team. Establish guidelines and provide team members with the resources they need to make ethical decisions and work towards sustainable outcomes.

3. **Accountability and responsibility**: Assign specific roles and responsibilities for maintaining ethical and sustainable practices within the project. This promotes accountability and ensures that the entire team is working together to achieve ECCSR objectives.

4. **Monitoring and evaluation**: Regularly review and assess the project's progress towards its ECCSR goals, using established KPIs and performance metrics. Address any deviations from the plan and take corrective action where necessary.

5. **Stakeholder engagement**: Involve stakeholders in the monitoring and control process, ensuring they have access to relevant

information and can provide feedback on the project's ethical and sustainable performance.

6. **Foster a collaborative culture**: Encourage team members to work together and share ideas, promoting a collaborative environment that supports ethical decision-making and sustainable outcomes. Provide opportunities for cross-functional collaboration and knowledge sharing to help drive innovation and problem-solving.

7. **Celebrate successes**: Recognise and reward team members for their contributions to the project's ECCSR objectives. This can help to reinforce the importance of ethical collaboration and sustainable results, motivating the team to continue working towards these goals.

8. **Continuous improvement**: Use the monitoring and control phase to identify areas for improvement in ECCSR performance. Implement lessons learned and best practices from previous projects, and encourage team members to share their own experiences and suggestions for improvement.

Specific examples:

1. **London 2012 Olympics**: The London Olympics organising committee focused on sustainability from the planning phase through to execution. They incorporated eco-friendly building materials, promoted the use of public transportation, and minimised waste during the event. They also ensured ethical labour practices and prioritised local suppliers to support the local economy.

2. **The High Line in New York City**: This public park was created by converting an abandoned elevated railway line into a green urban space. The project prioritised sustainability by using native plants, incorporating energy-efficient lighting, and promoting eco-friendly transportation options such as walking and cycling. The project team worked closely with the local community to ensure the park

met their needs and expectations, demonstrating a commitment to ethical collaboration.

By focusing on ECCSR throughout the project execution process, a project manager can ensure the project not only meets its objectives but also contributes positively to the environment, society, and the organisation's reputation.

8.2 Assembling your Project Team

Creating and managing effective project teams is critical to the success of any project. A project team is a group of individuals with complementary skills and experience who work together to achieve project goals. Effective project teams are characterized by strong communication, collaboration, and a shared sense of purpose. In this article, we will explore some best practices for creating and managing effective project teams, drawing on current literature and citing useful resources.

8.2.1   Define Roles and Responsibilities

Defining clear roles and responsibilities is critical to creating and managing effective project teams. Each team member should have a clearly defined role that aligns with their skills and experience. This helps to ensure that everyone is working towards the same goals and avoids duplication of effort. Additionally, it is important to define who is responsible for each task or activity in the project, which helps to ensure that tasks are completed on time and within budget.

8.2.2   Foster Collaboration and Communication

Collaboration and communication are essential components of effective project teams. Project managers should create a culture of openness and transparency that encourages team members to share ideas and feedback. This can be achieved through regular team meetings, status updates, and other forms of communication. Additionally, project managers should encourage team members to work collaboratively and share knowledge and expertise to achieve project goals.

8.2.3   Build Trust and Respect

Building trust and respect among team members is critical to creating and managing effective project teams. Project managers should establish clear expectations for behavior and conduct regular team-building activities to help team members get to know each other better. Additionally, project managers should recognize and reward team members for their contributions, which helps to build a sense of trust and respect among team members.

8.2.4 Develop and Manage Skills

Developing and managing skills is an important part of creating and managing effective project teams. Project managers should provide team members with the training and resources they need to perform their roles effectively. Additionally, project managers should provide regular feedback and performance evaluations to help team members identify areas for improvement and develop new skills.

8.2.5 Manage Conflict

Managing conflict is an important part of creating and managing effective project teams. Project managers should establish clear conflict resolution procedures and encourage team members to raise any issues or concerns they may have. Additionally, project managers should work to resolve conflicts quickly and fairly to avoid negative impacts on the project.

8.2.6 Celebrate Success

Celebrating success is an important part of creating and managing effective project teams. Project managers should recognize and celebrate the achievements of the team and individual team members. This helps to build a sense of accomplishment and satisfaction among team members and encourages them to continue to work towards project goals.

8.2.7 Useful Resources on team management

There are a variety of resources available for team managers looking to learn more about creating and managing effective project teams. Here are a few up-to-date resources that team managers may find useful:

8.2.7.1 Project Management Institute (PMI)

The PMI is a professional association for project managers that offers a variety of resources, including training, certifications, and best practices for managing quality in projects. Their website is at https://www.pmi.org/ .

8.2.7.2 Harvard Business Review

Harvard Business Review is a leading business publication that offers articles and insights on a variety of topics, including team management and leadership. Their website is at https://hbr.org/ .

8.2.7.3 ProjectManager.com

ProjectManager.com is a cloud-based project management software that offers a variety of tools and resources for managing projects and teams.

8.2.8 The Sales Conference - Team

The team behind a sales conference is the thing that above all else makes it run like magic, or become an unwieldy mess.

Specifying clear roles and responsibilities ensures that all the jobs get done as someone is specifically tasked with each one.

Having a couple of general helpers can be very useful as unexpected stuff always crops up so some unassigned helpers to give these last minute tasks to always makes the process smoother.

In the short term, autocratic leadership might seem to get stuff done faster, but creating a sense of camaraderie, that everyone is working together in a team to create something fabulous, is a much more ethical, sustainable and successful approach.

Work together, eliminate hierarchy, draw on everyone's diverse experiences and skillsets, and constantly harvest ideas from the team to better the event. I try to always make a note of great ideas and who came up with them, and then at the end of the project, when we have the party to celebrate success, I have talking points for everyone to showcase their contributions to the end result.

8.3 Project Quality Management

Quality management is the process of ensuring that a project meets or exceeds the expectations of stakeholders in terms of quality, functionality, and performance. In modern project management, quality management is an essential component of project success. In this article, we will explore some best practices for quality management in modern project management, drawing on current literature and citing useful resources.

8.3.1 Define Quality Standards

Defining quality standards is the first step in quality management. Project managers should work with stakeholders to define clear quality standards that outline the expectations for the project in terms of quality, functionality, and performance. This helps to ensure that everyone is working towards the same goals and avoids confusion and misunderstandings.

8.3.2 Plan Quality Control

Planning quality control is an important part of quality management. Project managers should develop a plan for quality control that outlines the processes and procedures that will be used to ensure that the project meets the defined quality standards. This may include testing, inspections, and other quality control measures.

8.3.3 Monitor Quality Performance

Monitoring quality performance is critical to quality management. Project managers should monitor the quality of the project throughout its lifecycle to ensure that it meets the defined quality standards. This can be achieved through regular quality control inspections, testing, and other measures.

8.3.4 Continuously Improve Quality

Continuously improving quality is an essential component of quality management. Project managers should work with stakeholders to identify opportunities for improvement and implement changes to improve quality, functionality, and performance. This may include process improvements, changes to the project plan, or other measures.

8.3.5 Manage Quality Risks

Managing quality risks is an important part of quality management. Project managers should identify potential quality risks and develop strategies to mitigate them. This may include developing contingency plans, allocating additional resources, or implementing additional quality control measures.

There are a variety of resources available for project managers looking to learn more about quality management. Here are a few up-to-date resources that project managers may find useful:

8.3.6 International Organization for Standardization (ISO)

ISO is a global standard-setting organization that offers a variety of standards related to quality management, including the ISO 9000 family of standards. Their website is at https://www.iso.org/ .

8.3.7 Project Management Institute (PMI)

The PMI is a professional association for project managers that offers a variety of resources, including training, certifications, and best practices for managing quality in projects. Their website is at https://www.pmi.org/ .

8.3.8 American Society for Quality (ASQ)

ASQ is a professional association for quality management professionals that offers a variety of resources, including training, certifications, and best practices for managing quality in projects. Their website is at https://asq.org/ .

Project Management made easy...

Quality Progress Magazine is a leading publication produced by the ASQ (above) for quality management professionals that offers articles and insights on a variety of topics related to quality management.

8.4 Communication Management

Communications management is the process of planning, executing, and controlling the flow of information related to a project. It involves creating and managing effective communication channels to ensure that information is shared among project stakeholders in a timely and effective manner. Effective communications management is critical to the success of any project, as it helps to ensure that all stakeholders are informed and engaged throughout the project lifecycle.

For an inexperienced project manager, effective communications management can be challenging. However, there are some best practices that can be followed to ensure that communications management is done effectively.

8.4.1 Define your project's communication goals

The first step in communications management is to define communication goals. Project managers should work with stakeholders to identify the communication needs of the project, including what information needs to be communicated, to whom, and when. This helps to ensure that everyone is working towards the same goals and avoids confusion and misunderstandings.

8.4.2 Develop a Communications Plan

Once communication goals have been defined, project managers should develop a communications plan. The plan should outline the processes and procedures that will be used to ensure that information is shared among project stakeholders in a timely and effective manner. This may include regular meetings, status updates, and other forms of communication.

8.4.3 Identify Communication Channels

Identifying the right communication channels is an important part of communications management. Project managers should identify the most effective communication channels for each stakeholder group, based on their preferences and needs. This may include email, phone, video conferencing, or other methods.

8.4.4   Manage Stakeholder Expectations

Managing stakeholder expectations is critical to effective communications management. Project managers should work to ensure that stakeholders are informed and engaged throughout the project lifecycle, and that their expectations are managed appropriately. This may involve providing regular updates, addressing concerns and issues in a timely manner, and ensuring that stakeholders are involved in key project decisions.

8.4.5   Monitor Communications Performance

Monitoring communications performance is an essential component of communications management. Project managers should regularly review the effectiveness of their communication channels and adjust them as needed to ensure that information is shared effectively among stakeholders.

There are resources available for project managers looking to learn more about communications management. Here are a couple that you may find useful:

8.4.6   Communicate Magazine

Communicate is a publication for communications professionals that offers articles and insights on a variety of topics related to communications management. Their website is at https://www.communicatemagazine.com/ .

8.4.7   Harvard Business Review

Project Management made easy...

Harvard Business Review is a leading business publication that offers articles and insights on a variety of topics, including communications management and leadership. The HBR website is at https://hbr.org/ .

8.4.8 The Sales Conference - Communication

Communications when organising, planning and then running and event is critically important.

There are many stakeholders, both inside and outside of your organization. Things are changing rapidly – plans need updating on a daily basis, speakers promise to show up them pull out, the venue suddenly has to move you to a different main room, the sales manager wants to move the order of presentations, the printers call to say theu can't get the brochures done in time.

Use one of the best parts of the agile project management framework - the daily stand-up meeting. This is a **really** good way to keep everybody updated and aware of everything else that's going on. You gather the team together ideally in the same room but this also works on zoom at a given time each morning and everybody has two minutes to tell the rest of the team three things.

1- what they did yesterday.

2 - What are they doing today

3 - Whatever is blocking them from achieving their objectives

The benefit of this quick update around the room is that everybody knows what everybody else is doing and has done ,and any issues that need help from somebody else have also been raised.

The daily stand up is not the place to resolve problems, but simply to highlight the problems exist and need resolving outside of the meeting.

It's one of the best ways to keep something like an event on track and moving and I know some event managers have daily stand ups, sometimes twice a day to ensure the communication flows are being maintained.

Another pretty useful thing is to have a Gantt chart of the different key tasks around the event, updated on a continual basis via a webpage that everybody has the link to.

Combine this with a specific email address that you as the project manager use for project communications that everybody needs to be aware of - for instance a change in the meeting room, or the order of presentations.

These are simple, but effective ways to ensure that communications is streamlined and that everybody stays on the same page and up-to-date with the ever changing circumstances of the project.

8.5 Change Management

Change management is an integral part of the project management process, as it encompasses the methodologies, tools, and strategies used to manage changes that occur throughout the project lifecycle. These changes may be triggered by factors such as shifting stakeholder requirements, new technological advancements, or modifications in the project's scope or objectives.

Effective change management is crucial to ensuring that projects remain on track and continue to deliver value to stakeholders, despite the inevitable uncertainties and challenges that may arise.

8.5.1 Why Change Management is so important in Project Management

Change management plays a critical role in project management for several reasons:

a. **Enhances adaptability**: Change management enables project teams to respond effectively to evolving project requirements and adapt to new circumstances, ensuring that the project remains aligned with stakeholder expectations and objectives.

b. **Reduces risk**: By proactively identifying, assessing, and addressing potential risks associated with changes, change management helps to minimize the likelihood of project disruptions, delays, or failures.

c. **Promotes stakeholder buy-in**: Effective change management engages stakeholders in the decision-making process, fostering a sense of ownership and commitment to the project's success.

d. **Preserves project value**: By ensuring that changes are carefully managed and aligned with project goals, change management helps to protect the overall value of the project and its deliverables.

8.5.2 Minimizing Fear and Resistance to Change

Resistance to change is a common challenge in project management, as changes can create feelings of uncertainty, fear, and anxiety among team members and stakeholders. To minimize fear and resistance, project managers should:

a. **Communicate openly and transparently**: Providing clear, consistent, and timely information about the nature of the changes, the reasons behind them, and their potential impact can help alleviate concerns and foster a sense of trust and understanding. Open and transparent communication can also dispel rumours and misinformation that might fuel resistance.

b. **Address emotional reactions**: Acknowledge the emotional impact of change on team members and stakeholders, and offer support to help them navigate their feelings. Providing a safe space for individuals to express their concerns, ask questions, and receive guidance can help reduce anxiety and promote acceptance of the changes.

c. **Demonstrate empathy**: Show empathy and understanding toward those who may be affected by the changes. By expressing genuine concern for their well-being and taking their perspectives into account, project managers can build rapport and minimize resistance.

d. **Offer training and support**: Providing team members with the necessary training and resources to adapt to the changes can help boost their confidence and competence, reducing fear and resistance.

8.5.3 Emotional Intelligence

In the context of creating communication plans and fostering team collaboration on projects, Goleman's Emotional Intelligence (EI) framework is highly applicable, as it can help project leaders optimise their leadership and maximise the effectiveness and efficiency of project teams. Goleman's framework consists of five key components: self-awareness, self-regulation, motivation, empathy, and social skills.

1. **Self-awareness:** This refers to the ability to understand one's own emotions, strengths, and weaknesses. A project leader with high self-awareness can effectively recognise their feelings and understand how they may impact their decision-making and communication. This skill enables the leader to create a communication plan that takes into account their own preferences and working style, as well as their team members' needs.

2. **Self-regulation:** The ability to control one's emotions and reactions is crucial in a project environment. A project leader who can self-regulate can adapt to changing circumstances, manage stress, and maintain a positive atmosphere within the team. This skill helps ensure that the communication plan is implemented effectively, even during challenging situations or when unexpected issues arise.

3. **Motivation:** A motivated project leader can inspire their team to work towards a common goal and stay focused on the project's objectives. By understanding what drives the team members, a leader can create a communication plan that keeps everyone engaged and motivated throughout the project. This can lead to increased efficiency and effectiveness in project execution.

4. **Empathy:** Empathy is the ability to understand and share the feelings of others. An empathetic project leader can anticipate the needs of their team members and stakeholders and address potential issues before they escalate. By incorporating empathy into the communication plan, a project leader can create an

environment of trust and open dialogue, which is essential for effective collaboration and decision-making.

5. **Social skills:** Effective communication and relationship-building are essential components of successful project management. A project leader with strong social skills can foster a collaborative environment where team members feel comfortable sharing their ideas and concerns. By using these skills to develop a communication plan, a project leader can ensure that all stakeholders are kept informed and engaged, ultimately leading to a more successful project outcome.

In conclusion, Goleman's Emotional Intelligence framework can be effectively used by project leaders to create communication plans and foster collaboration within project teams. By incorporating the principles of self-awareness, self-regulation, motivation, empathy, and social skills into their leadership style, project leaders can enhance the efficiency and effectiveness of their teams, leading to more successful project outcomes.

8.5.4 Kotter's 8 steps of Change

Kotter's Eight Steps of Change Management is a widely recognised methodology that helps leaders produce lasting change in their organisations. The up-to-date model includes eight stages that can be applied to project management, particularly when dealing with change during a project or changes brought about by a project. Here's an outline of Kotter's eight steps and their applicability to project management:

- CREATE A SENSE OF URGENCY
- BUILD A GUIDING COALITION
- FORM A STRATEGIC VISION
- ENLIST A VOLUNTEER ARMY
- ENABLE ACTION BY REMOVING BARRIERS
- GENERATE SHORT-TERM WINS
- SUSTAIN ACCELERATION
- INSTITUTE CHANGE

THE BIG opportunity

1. **Create** a sense of urgency: In project management, it's crucial to establish the importance of the project and the need for timely action. By creating a sense of urgency, project managers can motivate their teams and stakeholders to prioritise the project and be proactive in addressing challenges that may arise.

2. **Build** a guiding coalition: Forming a strong team of influential individuals who are committed to the project's success is essential. These individuals should have diverse skills and backgrounds to bring a range of perspectives and drive the project forward. In project management, this coalition can help navigate the complexities of the project and support decision-making processes.

3. **Form** a strategic vision and initiatives: Developing a clear vision and strategy for the project helps guide the team's actions and maintain focus on the project's objectives. This vision should be communicated effectively to the entire team and stakeholders to ensure alignment and commitment to the project's goals.

4. **Enlist** a volunteer army: In project management, it's essential to engage a broad range of people who are committed to the project's success. By enlisting a "volunteer army" of supporters, project managers can create a strong network of individuals who can contribute to the project, help overcome resistance to change, and promote the project's benefits.

5. **Enable** action by removing barriers: As a project progresses, there may be obstacles or barriers that impede the team's progress. Project managers should identify these barriers and take steps to remove them, enabling the team to work more efficiently and effectively in implementing the project's objectives.

6. **Generate** short-term wins: Celebrating short-term successes can help build momentum and maintain motivation within the project team. Project managers should identify milestones and achievements that demonstrate progress and celebrate these wins

with the team and stakeholders to keep everyone engaged and committed to the project.

7. **Sustain** acceleration: Change management in project management is an ongoing process. To sustain momentum, project managers must continually evaluate the project's progress, adjust the strategy as needed, and ensure the team remains focused on the project's objectives. This includes providing ongoing support, resources, and encouragement to the project team.

8. **Institute** change: Lastly, project managers should work to embed the changes resulting from the project into the organisation's culture, processes, and structures. This ensures that the project's outcomes are sustained over the long term and that the benefits of the project are realised throughout the organisation.

More detail on Kotter's model and downloadable resources can be found at the Kotter International website - https://www.kotterinc.com/methodology/8-steps/

8.5.5 Involving Stakeholders in Consultative Discussions

Involving stakeholders in consultative discussions is essential for effective change management, as it helps to:

a. **Build trust and credibility**: Engaging stakeholders in the decision-making process demonstrates respect for their opinions and expertise, fostering trust and credibility between project managers and stakeholders.

b. **Identify potential issues and concerns**: Consultative discussions can help uncover potential challenges or concerns that may have been overlooked during the initial planning stages, allowing for more informed decision-making and better risk management.

c. **Generate buy-in and commitment**: By involving stakeholders in the change management process, project managers can create a sense of ownership and shared responsibility for the project's success. This collaboration can lead to increased commitment and support for the proposed changes, as stakeholders are more likely to embrace changes they have actively contributed to shaping.

d. **Tap into diverse perspectives**: Consultative discussions enable project managers to access a wealth of knowledge, experience, and ideas from different stakeholders. By incorporating these diverse perspectives, project managers can develop more comprehensive and effective change management strategies.

e. **Facilitate smoother implementation**: When stakeholders have a clear understanding of the changes and their rationale, they are more likely to support and participate in the implementation process. This collaborative approach can lead to fewer obstacles and a smoother transition during the execution of the changes.

8.5.6 The Necessity for Proactive Action in Managing Change

Proactive action is essential in change management, as it allows project managers to anticipate and address potential issues before they escalate into significant problems. Some key aspects of proactive change management include:

a. **Continuously monitoring the project environment**: Regularly assess the project's internal and external environment for potential changes, risks, or opportunities. This ongoing monitoring enables project managers to identify potential issues early, allowing for a more agile and adaptive response.

b. **Developing contingency plans**: Proactively develop contingency plans to address potential changes, risks, or disruptions. Having these plans in place ensures that project managers can quickly and effectively respond to unexpected events, minimizing their impact on the project.

c. **Building a change-ready culture**: Foster a culture of adaptability, resilience, and continuous learning within the project team. Encourage team members to embrace change as an opportunity for growth and improvement, and provide them with the skills, resources, and support needed to adapt to new situations.

d. **Engaging stakeholders early and often**: Regularly involve stakeholders in the change management process, soliciting their input and feedback, and keeping them informed about project developments. This proactive engagement helps to build trust, identify potential issues, and foster buy-in for the changes.

9 Project Monitoring and Controlling

Project monitoring and control is a critical stage in project management, and it involves tracking the progress of the project and making adjustments as needed to ensure that it stays on track.

For beginners in project management, the monitoring and control stage can seem overwhelming. There are many different factors to consider, including timelines, budgets, resources, and team dynamics. However, with the right approach and tools, this stage can be manageable and even enjoyable.

One key approach to monitoring and control is to use a project management tool, such as a Gantt chart or a project management software program. These tools can help project managers to track progress, identify issues, and make adjustments as needed. They can also help to communicate the status of the project to stakeholders, which is critical for ensuring that everyone is on the same page.

Another approach to monitoring and control is to establish regular check-ins with the project team and stakeholders. This can include weekly or bi-weekly status meetings, where team members can provide updates on their progress and identify any issues or concerns. These meetings can also be used to brainstorm solutions and make adjustments to the project plan as needed.

It's also important for project managers to be proactive in monitoring and controlling the project. This means staying on top of deadlines, budgets, and resources, and taking action as soon as issues arise. By being proactive, project managers can ensure that the project stays on track and that any issues are addressed before they become major problems. Let's see how to address some of these issues in a bit more detail…

9.1 Project Performance Monitoring

Performance monitoring involves tracking the progress of the project to ensure that it stays on track and meets quality standards. Without effective performance monitoring, projects can quickly fall behind schedule, go over budget, or fail to meet the expectations of stakeholders.

For beginners in project management, performance monitoring can seem like a daunting task. However, with the right approach, it can be manageable and even enjoyable. One key approach to performance monitoring is to establish clear performance metrics for the project. This might include timelines, budgets, quality standards, or other factors that are important to the success of the project.

Once these metrics have been established, it's important to track them regularly and make adjustments as needed. This might involve weekly or bi-weekly check-ins with the project team to review progress, identify any issues or concerns, and brainstorm solutions. It might also involve using project management tools, such as a Gantt chart or a project management software program, to track progress and communicate the status of the project to stakeholders.

Another key approach to performance monitoring is to establish a culture of accountability within the project team. This means holding team members responsible for their individual contributions to the project and ensuring that everyone is aware of their responsibilities and the expectations for the project. By creating a culture of accountability, project managers can help to ensure that everyone is working together towards the same goals and that the project stays on track.

9.2   The Project Change Control Process

As discussed earlier in the scoping of a project, it's important for projects to keep control over scope creep. Few projects ever occur where requests for change don't come in on a pretty constant basis, so putting in an effective process for filtering and deciding which changes should be allowed in is key in keeping a project on track.

The first step is to have the "3 Yes's then a No" conversation that I outline on page 53. But this leaves the onus on you as the project manager to make decisions and field such requests. In a more organised project environment, change requests on projects that have already been scoped are normally submitted as formal documents to a management board for review and acceptance. This is much better as it formalises the process, removes the responsibility from you as the project manager to decide on what changes will be added to the project, and ultimately frees up your time and energy to focus on delivery rather than constant interruptions and requests for additions.

Managing change requests in a project environment can be a challenge, but it's an important part of project control. Change requests can come from a variety of sources, including stakeholders, team members, and external factors. To effectively manage change requests, project managers need to have a clear process in place that allows them to assess the impact of the change, decide whether or not to accept it, and implement the change if necessary.

An effective process for managing change requests is the following:

1. **Identify the change request**: The first step is to identify the change request and gather information about it. This might involve speaking with the person who submitted the request, reviewing project documentation, or conducting a feasibility study to assess the impact of the change.

2. **Assess the impact**: The next step is to assess the impact of the change on the project. This might include considering the time, cost, and resource implications of the change, as well as any potential risks or benefits.

3. **Decide whether to accept or reject the change request**: Based on the assessment of the change request, the project manager (or management team) needs to make a decision about whether to accept or reject it. This decision should be based on the impact of the change on the project goals, timelines, and budget.

4. **Implement the change if necessary**: If the change request is accepted, the project manager needs to implement the change and update the project plan and schedule as needed. This might involve reallocating resources, adjusting timelines, or revising the project budget.

5. **Communicate the decision**: Finally, it's important to communicate the decision about the change request to all relevant stakeholders. This might involve updating the project team, informing external stakeholders, or revising project documentation to reflect the change.

The Stage-Gate Process

The Stage-Gate process, introduced by Robert Cooper in his best-selling book *"Winning at new Products: Creating Value through innovation"* (Amazon link https://amzn.to/3yCZjDJ), is a widely used approach to managing change in a project environment. This process involves breaking the project down into distinct stages, or "gates," each of which represents a milestone in the project's progress.

At each gate, the project team evaluates the progress of the project and makes decisions about whether to proceed to the next stage or to make changes to the project plan.

The reason that the Stage-Gate process has become so globally recognised as best practice is that the default for a Stage-Gate meeting is NOT to let projects continue. Cooper calls this "gates with teeth".

Although such an approach can be challenging, particularly for organisations who haven't followed good project management change processes previously, applying positive filters on projects continuing results in far better and more efficient allocation of resources aimed at projects that continue to deliver high return on investment potential.

There's many reasons for a project not getting through a Stage-Gate review. The project team may not be performing to expectations, although this is quite rare as a result for a project hold or stop.

More common would be external changes in the corporate environment perhaps. A downturn in demand for the product that is being produced by the project might result in the project are no longer having as attractive a return on investment potential. A regulatory change might render the project no longer required or viable. Or simply a change in direction of company, policy or strategy might result in projects underway being reviewed and stopped or put on hold as the company redirects its efforts.

Using Stage-Gate is a very practical and positive way to optimise the utilisation of what are always scarce resources within a company. Be these people equipment, time, money or anything else that is required to make a project happen..

The Stage-Gate process can be applied to projects of all sizes and types, and it provides a structured approach to change control. The key steps in the Stage-Gate process are as follows:

9.2.1   Idea Generation

The first stage of the process is to generate ideas for the project. This might involve brainstorming sessions, market research, or customer feedback.

9.2.2   Idea Screening

Once the ideas have been generated, they need to be screened to determine their feasibility and potential impact on the project. This might involve evaluating the ideas against a set of criteria or conducting a feasibility study.

9.2.3   Concept Development

The next stage is to develop a concept for the project based on the selected idea. This might involve creating a detailed project plan, developing a business case, or conducting a risk assessment.

9.2.4   Business Analysis

In this stage, the project team evaluates the potential impact of the project on the business, including its financial implications, impact on existing processes, and overall alignment with the organization's goals.

9.2.5   Project Development

Once the business case has been approved, the project development stage begins. This might involve developing prototypes, creating detailed project plans, or conducting further research and development.

9.2.6 Testing and Validation

In this stage, the project team tests the project to ensure that it meets the specified requirements and is aligned with the organization's goals.

9.2.7 Launch

The final stage of the process is to launch the project, which might involve a formal launch event, product release, or other form of launch activity.

More on Stage-Gate at Stage-Gate International - https://www.stage-gate.com/

The Stage-Gate process provides a structured approach to managing change in a project environment, and it can be applied to projects of all sizes and types. By breaking the project down into distinct stages and evaluating progress at each gate, project managers can ensure that the project stays on track and meets the expectations of stakeholders.

9.3 Irrational escalation of commitment

"Irrational escalation of commitment", also known as "commitment bias" is a concept from psychology that has significant implications for project management, especially when using Robert Cooper's Stage-Gate process. The term refers to situations where people make irrational decisions based on rational decisions from the past or to justify actions already taken. In other words, it's when we get too attached to a project or decision, even when evidence suggests it might not be the best course of action.

In the context of project management and Cooper's Stage-Gate process, irrational escalation can occur when project teams and managers become too committed to a project, even when it's no longer viable or meeting its objectives. The Stage-Gate process is designed to help organizations make informed decisions about whether to continue or terminate projects at various checkpoints or "gates" throughout the project lifecycle.

Irrational escalation of commitment can hinder the effectiveness of the Stage-Gate process by making it harder for project teams to objectively evaluate a project's progress and decide whether to move forward or not. For example, if a team has invested a lot of time and resources in a project, they may be more likely to justify continuing it, even when the data shows that it's not meeting expectations or has a low likelihood of success.

To mitigate irrational escalation of commitment in the Stage-Gate process, project managers should:

1. Establish clear criteria for evaluating projects at each gate. This can help ensure that decisions are based on objective data and not just the emotional attachment to a project.

2. Encourage open communication and feedback within the project team. This can help to create an environment where team members

feel comfortable expressing their concerns about a project's progress without fear of retribution.

3. Foster a culture that embraces change and adaptability. By encouraging team members to be open to new ideas and willing to change course when necessary, it's less likely that they'll become too attached to a particular project or decision.

4. Periodically review and assess the project's progress and adjust the goals as needed. This can help to ensure that the project remains aligned with the organization's strategic objectives and is on track for success.

By being aware of irrational escalation of commitment and taking steps to address it, project managers can make better decisions when using the Stage-Gate process and increase the likelihood of a project's success.

A reference to learn more about this psychological term is available on The Decision Lab's website:

- The Decision Lab: Commitment Bias URL: https://thedecisionlab.com/biases/commitment-bias

This source provides insights into how commitment bias can affect decision-making in various contexts, including organizational environments. By understanding this concept, project managers can be better equipped to recognize and address the potential pitfalls associated with irrational escalation of commitment in their projects.

9.4 Project Risk Monitoring and Control

Risk monitoring and control is an essential part of any project management plan, and it involves identifying potential risks, assessing their likelihood and impact, and implementing strategies to manage and mitigate them.

9.4.1 Step 1: Identify Risks

The first step in the risk management process is to identify potential risks. This can be done through brainstorming sessions with the project team, reviewing past projects, and consulting with external stakeholders. Risks can be categorized into different types, such as technical risks, organizational risks, and financial risks.

9.4.2 Step 2: Assess Risks

Once the risks have been identified, they are assessed in terms of their likelihood and impact on the project. This helps to prioritize the risks and determine which ones require immediate attention. The Project Management Book of Knowledge recommends using a risk matrix to assess risks, which involves assigning a likelihood and impact score to each risk.

9.4.3 Step 3: Develop Risk Responses

After the risks have been assessed, strategies are developed to manage and mitigate them. This might involve developing contingency plans, allocating resources to address the risks, or making changes to the project plan to minimize the impact of the risks. The PRINCE2 methodology recommends developing risk responses based on four categories: avoid, transfer, mitigate, or accept.

9.4.4 Step 4: Monitor Risks

Throughout the project, the risks are monitored and reviewed to ensure that the strategies are working effectively. The Project Management

Book of Knowledge recommends using a risk register to track the status of each risk, including the risk response and any changes that have been made to the project plan.

9.4.5   The Risk Register

A risk register is a tool used to identify, assess, and track potential risks to a project. The risk register helps to ensure that potential risks are identified early, and appropriate responses are planned and implemented to mitigate or avoid those risks.

The risk register typically includes a list of identified risks, along with information about the risk, such as the likelihood and impact of the risk occurring, as well as the risk response plan.

The risk response plan outlines the actions that will be taken to address the risk, should it occur.

The risk register should be regularly reviewed and updated throughout the project to ensure that new risks are identified and managed appropriately.

Project Management made easy...

Here's an example of a simple risk register:

Risk ID	Risk Description	Likelihood	Impact	Risk Response Plan
001	Delayed delivery of project materials	High	High	Work with supplier to expedite delivery; identify alternative suppliers
002	Key team member unavailable due to illness	Medium	High	Identify backup resources; adjust project schedule as necessary
003	Change in project scope	Low	High	Document change request and assess impact on project schedule and budget
004	Unexpected cost overruns	High	Medium	Monitor project costs closely; adjust project budget and schedule as necessary

Likelihood and Impact are shown here as high, medium or low, but you can also score these on a 1 to 5 or 1 to 10 scale. This gives a little more granularity to separating high medium and low risks and allows for easier prioritisation.

Typically, most risk registers using numeric, scoring for likelihood and impact would have a column for overall risk score where the likelihood and impact scores were multiplied. The resulting score gives an overall risk score and then gives management teams, a clear priority list.

Starting with the highest risk scores, management can decide on relevant actions until they run out of time resources to put into risk management at which point the lowest scoring risks are typically just left noted, but without any specific actions to be taken.

9.4.5.1 Example - Burj Khalifa Hotel

One example of successful risk management in a project is the construction of the Burj Khalifa in Dubai. This project, which was the tallest building in the world at the time of its completion, involved numerous risks related to the design, construction, and operation of the building. To manage these risks, the project team employed a range of strategies, including developing detailed plans and contingency measures, using advanced construction technology, and conducting extensive testing and validation.

9.4.5.2 Example - NASA Mars Rover

Another example is the NASA Mars Rover project, which involved numerous risks related to the complex technology involved, the harsh environment of Mars, and the long distance between Earth and Mars. To manage these risks, the project team employed a range of strategies, including developing backup systems, conducting extensive testing and validation, and using remote operation to control the rover from Earth.

9.5 Project Status Reporting

Project status reporting is a means of providing regular updates to stakeholders about the project's progress, key achievements, milestones, and any issues that need to be addressed.

There are different ways to approach project status reporting, but the key is to find a method that works best for your team and stakeholders.

One common approach is to use a project status report, which is typically a document that summarizes the project's progress, issues, and risks. The report may also include information on budget and resource utilization, upcoming milestones, and any changes to the project plan.

Another option for project status reporting is to hold regular team meetings, such as weekly or biweekly check-ins. These meetings provide an opportunity for team members to share updates on their progress, discuss any issues, and collaborate on solutions.

For stakeholders who may not be directly involved in the project, but still have a vested interest in its success, it may be helpful to use visual aids such as dashboards, charts, or graphs. These tools provide a quick and easy way for stakeholders to see the project's progress at a glance.

Regardless of the approach taken, the key to effective project status reporting is to be consistent, clear, and concise. Regular communication ensures that everyone is on the same page and can address any issues or concerns in a timely manner. By keeping stakeholders informed, project managers can build trust, ensure accountability, and increase the likelihood of a successful outcome.

9.5.1 The 4-box approach – project status on a page

The four-box approach is a popular method for project status reporting that is used by many organizations. It involves dividing the project's progress into four boxes, each representing a different aspect of the project. The boxes typically include:

Accomplishments: This box summarizes the tasks that have been completed since the last report. It should provide specific details about what was achieved and how it contributes to the overall project.

Current Activities: This box outlines the tasks that are currently underway. It should provide a detailed breakdown of what is being worked on, who is responsible for each task, and when they are expected to be completed.

Issues/Concerns: This box highlights any challenges or obstacles that the project team is currently facing. It should provide a brief description of the issue, its impact on the project, and what is being done to resolve it.

Next Steps: This box outlines the tasks that are planned for the next reporting period. It should provide a clear description of what will be done, who will be responsible, and when it is expected to be completed.

It allows stakeholders to quickly understand the project's progress and any issues that need to be addressed. The approach is often combined with other reporting methods, such as Gantt charts or dashboards, to provide a comprehensive overview of the project's performance.

9.5.2 Project dashboards

A good site to look at this type of software is the 10 Best Project Management Dashboard Software Of 2023

at https://thedigitalprojectmanager.com/tools/project-management-dashboard-software/

10 Project Closure

Project closure is an essential part of the project management process. It is the final stage of a project where the project manager and the team evaluate the project's success and take necessary actions to complete the project formally. In other words, it's the time to put a stamp on a project and declare it finished.

The project closure process involves several activities, such as verifying that all project objectives are achieved, ensuring all project deliverables are completed and accepted by the client, collecting and archiving project documentation, and releasing project resources.

It's also the time to celebrate the project team's success, recognize team members' contributions, and thank them for their hard work.

Project closure is important because it allows the project team to evaluate the project's outcome and analyse what went right and wrong. It also provides an opportunity to review and document lessons learned so that they can be applied to future projects. Additionally, the project closure process ensures that all contractual obligations are fulfilled and all resources are released.

10.1 Applying ECCSR to the Closing phase

In the project closing process, a project manager can continue to apply ECCSR (ethical collaboration creating sustainable results) concepts to ensure that the project leaves a lasting positive impact. Here are some practical examples of incorporating ECCSR during the project closing phase:

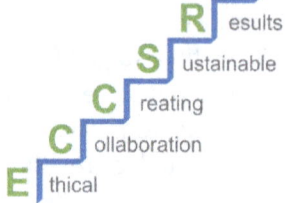

1. **Conduct a thorough project review**: Evaluate the project's performance against its ECCSR objectives by examining ethical and sustainable practices throughout its lifecycle. Identify areas of success and areas that need improvement, and use this information to inform future projects.

2. **Share knowledge and lessons learned**: Document and share the ethical and sustainability-related experiences, best practices, and lessons learned from the project with your team, organisation, and industry peers. This encourages ongoing improvement and ensures that the knowledge gained from the project is put to good use in future endeavours.

3. **Stakeholder feedback**: Gather feedback from stakeholders, including team members, clients, suppliers, and the local community, to assess the project's ethical and sustainable performance. Use their insights to make improvements and ensure better collaboration in future projects.

4. **Post-project sustainability**: Ensure that the project's outcomes continue to generate sustainable results even after the project is completed. This may involve planning for long-term maintenance, monitoring, or follow-up activities that promote ongoing environmental or social benefits.

5. **Recognise and celebrate achievements**: Acknowledge the project team's efforts and successes in achieving ECCSR objectives. Celebrating these accomplishments helps to reinforce the importance of ethical collaboration and sustainable results and motivates the team for future projects.

Specific examples:

1. **The Global Reporting Initiative (GRI)**: This independent international organisation develops sustainability reporting standards to help businesses, governments, and other organisations measure and communicate their economic, environmental, and social impacts. When closing a project, a project manager can use GRI's framework to assess the project's ECCSR performance and share the results with stakeholders. This transparency and communication can lead to better ethical collaboration and sustainable results in future projects.

   The GRI Initiative website is at
   https://www.globalreporting.org/

2. **Hurricane Katrina recovery projects**: Following the devastation of Hurricane Katrina in 2005, several rebuilding projects aimed to create sustainable and resilient communities in the affected areas. During the project closing phase, evaluations were conducted to assess the effectiveness of these efforts, including the impact on local communities and the environment. The lessons learned have been used to inform future disaster recovery efforts, promoting ethical collaboration and sustainable results.

By focusing on ECCSR during the project closing process, a project manager can ensure that the project's positive impact continues even after its completion. Incorporating ethical collaboration and sustainable results into the project closing phase can lead to long-term benefits for the environment, society, and the organisation's reputation.

10.2 Doing a Lessons Learned Review

Lessons learned is an important process in project management. It involves reviewing a project to identify what worked well, what didn't work well, and what could be improved for future projects. The purpose of conducting a lessons learned review is to capture and analyse insights and knowledge gained throughout a project, and to use that knowledge to improve future project outcomes.

To generate a lessons learned analysis, a process can be followed. This process typically includes five steps: identify, document, analyse, store, and retrieve. In the identification phase, the project team identifies key lessons that can be learned from the project. This may involve gathering feedback from stakeholders or reviewing project documentation.

In the **documentation** phase, the lessons identified are recorded in a formal report or document. This report typically includes details about what worked well and what didn't work well, as well as recommendations for improvement.

Next, in the **analysis** phase, the lessons documented are analysed and synthesized to identify patterns and insights. The goal of this phase is to identify themes and key takeaways that can be used to improve future projects.

Once the lessons are analysed, they should be **stored** and made accessible for future reference. This can involve storing them in a database, a project management software, or a shared document repository.

Finally, the **retrieved** phase involves using the lessons learned to improve future projects. This may involve incorporating the lessons learned into project plans, processes, or training materials.

10.2.1 Lessons from the trenches – the After Action Review

The After Action Report (AAR) is a type of review used by many military units to assess and learn from projects. It is a structured approach to analyse ing an operation or activity in order to identify what worked well and what could be improved upon.

The AAR process typically involves a debriefing session where participants discuss the event and share their observations and experiences. This information is then compiled into a report that includes recommendations for future improvement.

The AAR process has been adapted for use in project management, where it can be a valuable tool for identifying and addressing project issues. By conducting an AAR at the end of a project, project managers can identify successes and areas for improvement, as well as develop best practices that can be applied to future projects.

The AAR report should include an overview of the project, a summary of the event being reviewed, and an analysis of what went well and what did not. It should also include recommendations for improvements that can be implemented in future projects.

Remember, the purpose of the AAR is not to assign blame or criticism, but rather to identify opportunities for growth and learning. A conversational tone can be helpful in promoting an open and collaborative environment for sharing feedback and ideas.

Useful articles on this tool can be found at the following links:

1. https://www.mindtools.com/ap0ri1f/after-action-review-aar-process
2. https://hbr.org/2005/07/learning-in-the-thick-of-it

10.2.2 Start Stop Continue

The Start-Stop-Continue approach is a simple yet effective feedback and reflection tool used in various settings, including project management.

Although the specific origins of this approach are not clear, it is widely adopted due to its simplicity and effectiveness in identifying areas for improvement and facilitating continuous learning within teams.

In the context of project closure, the Start-Stop-Continue approach can be applied to after-action reviews (AARs) to evaluate the project's performance, identify lessons learned, and enhance future project management practices. Here's how this approach can be applied to project closure:

1. **Start**: During the AAR, the project team identifies new actions, processes, or behaviours that should be implemented in future projects. This could include introducing new communication tools, adopting a new project management methodology, or integrating a more rigorous risk assessment process. By discussing these "start" actions, the team can continuously improve its performance and increase the likelihood of success in future projects.

2. **Stop**: The team also reviews any actions, processes, or behaviours that were ineffective, counterproductive, or led to undesirable outcomes during the project. These "stop" actions might include discontinuing a particular reporting method, eliminating unnecessary meetings, or ceasing to use an outdated software tool. Identifying and addressing these issues helps prevent similar problems from arising in future projects and contributes to the team's overall development.

3. **Continue**: Lastly, the project team identifies successful actions, processes, or behaviours that contributed to the project's success and should be maintained in future projects. These "continue" actions might involve retaining a specific communication protocol, preserving a decision-making process, or maintaining a certain level of stakeholder engagement. By highlighting and reinforcing these positive practices, the team can ensure that they are carried forward into future projects.

When using the Start-Stop-Continue approach in AARs, it's crucial to assign an owner and a deadline to each action to ensure timely implementation and accountability.

Once the AAR is complete, the agreed-upon actions should be communicated to all team members, so everyone is aware of the improvements and adjustments to be made in future projects.

10.3 Project Deliverables Acceptance

When nearing the end of a project, it is important to have a clear process in place for accepting project deliverables. Acceptance of project deliverables signifies the completion of the project and it ensures that the work meets the requirements set out in the project plan.

The acceptance process should be clearly defined and communicated to all stakeholders involved in the project. This process typically involves a review of the deliverables to ensure they meet the standards and criteria set out in the project plan. This review should be done by all parties involved in the project including the project team, the project manager, and the stakeholders.

One common approach is to use a formal acceptance document, which outlines the criteria for acceptance and the process for reviewing and approving deliverables. This document should also include a sign-off section, where stakeholders can formally approve the deliverables once they have been reviewed and accepted.

It is important to ensure that all stakeholders are involved in the acceptance process and that they have a clear understanding of the criteria for acceptance. This helps to minimize the risk of misunderstandings and ensures that everyone is working towards the same goal.

In addition, it is important to communicate the acceptance process early on in the project to ensure that everyone is aware of the expectations and standards for deliverables. This helps to avoid any surprises or misunderstandings later on in the project.

Overall, the acceptance process is an important step in the project management process, as it ensures that the project deliverables meet the requirements set out in the project plan and that all stakeholders are satisfied with the outcome of the project.

10.4 Project Closure Checklist

A project closure checklist is a crucial tool that can help ensure a smooth and successful end to a project. By creating and following a project closure checklist, project managers can make sure that all the necessary steps are taken before closing out the project. This can help ensure that any loose ends are tied up, all stakeholders are satisfied, and that the project's goals and objectives have been met.

There are many benefits to creating a project closure checklist. For one, it can help ensure that all necessary tasks have been completed, and that all relevant stakeholders have been informed of the project's completion. This can help prevent any misunderstandings or miscommunications down the line. Additionally, by having a clear and comprehensive project closure checklist, project managers can ensure that they are not missing any key steps or tasks, which can help prevent delays or complications.

To create a project closure checklist, project managers should start by reviewing the project's objectives and goals, as well as any contractual or regulatory requirements. From there, they should identify all the necessary tasks that need to be completed before the project can be officially closed out, such as finalizing documentation, completing any necessary training or handoffs, and conducting a final review of the project's performance.

Once the necessary tasks have been identified, project managers should create a checklist or document that outlines each task, along with any associated deadlines or dependencies. This checklist should be shared with all relevant stakeholders, and should be updated as tasks are completed or new tasks are identified.

Overall, creating a project closure checklist can help ensure that projects are closed out successfully, with all necessary tasks completed and all stakeholders informed. By taking the time to create a comprehensive and detailed checklist, project managers can help prevent any last-minute surprises or complications, and can ensure that their projects are completed on time and on budget.

Here is an example of a project closure checklist that can be used as a guide, although it's important to note that every project scenario is different, so this general guide will probably need tweaking:

1. Ensure that all project deliverables have been completed and signed off by stakeholders.

2. Confirm that all project documentation has been finalized, including project plans, schedules, budgets, and risk management plans.

3. Verify that all outstanding issues and risks have been addressed and resolved.

4. Conduct a lessons learned review to capture any insights and recommendations for future projects.

5. Obtain final approval and sign off from the project sponsor.

6. Complete a final budget reconciliation to ensure that all expenses have been accounted for.

7. Archive all project documentation in a secure and accessible location.

8. Communicate project closure to all stakeholders, including project team members and external partners.

9. Celebrate project success and recognize team members for their contributions.

10. Conduct a post-project review with the project team to discuss achievements, challenges, and opportunities for improvement.

10.5 Project Evaluation

At the end of a project, it's important to evaluate how the project went. This helps you learn from your successes and failures, and improve your project management skills for future projects. The evaluation process usually involves reviewing the project's goals and objectives, assessing how well those were met, and identifying any areas for improvement.

To evaluate a project, you can use a variety of tools such as project reviews, surveys, and stakeholder feedback. Project reviews involve assessing the project's performance against the plan, such as the schedule, budget, and quality. Surveys can be used to gather feedback from team members and stakeholders about their perceptions of the project's success, and any areas for improvement. Stakeholder feedback can be obtained by conducting meetings or interviews with key stakeholders, such as the project sponsor or customer.

Overall, the evaluation process helps you to learn from your experiences, make improvements for future projects, and ensure that your organization continues to improve its project management skills. By evaluating your projects, you can identify what worked well, what didn't work so well, and how you can improve your project management skills for future projects.

10.6 Knowledge Transfer

Knowledge transfer is an important part of project management, as it helps to ensure that knowledge and skills are shared among team members and other stakeholders, and that valuable insights and best practices are not lost. Here are a few ways that knowledge transfer can be facilitated:

1. **Regular team meetings**: One of the simplest and most effective ways to facilitate knowledge transfer is to hold regular team meetings, where team members can share updates, discuss challenges, and offer insights and ideas. This can help to ensure that everyone is on the same page, and that valuable information is not missed.

2. **Knowledge sharing platforms**: Another approach is to use online platforms or tools that allow team members to share information, documents, and ideas. This can include tools like wikis, shared folders, and project management software, which can make it easy for team members to access and collaborate on project-related information.

3. **Mentorship and coaching**: Another effective approach is to pair team members with mentors or coaches, who can help to guide and support them, and share their own knowledge and experience. This can help to build skills and confidence among team members, and ensure that knowledge and best practices are passed down from more experienced team members.

4. **External consultants and experts**: In some cases, it may be necessary to bring in outside consultants or experts to help with specific aspects of the project. This can be a valuable way to transfer knowledge and skills, as these experts can share their experience and insights with the project team, and help to build capacity for future projects.

Overall, the key to successful knowledge transfer is to create a culture of collaboration and learning within the project team, and to be intentional and proactive about sharing information and best practices. By doing so, you can help to ensure that your project is a success, and that your team members are equipped with the skills and knowledge they need to tackle future challenges.

10.7 Celebrating achievements & team recognition

Celebrating achievements and recognizing the efforts of team members is an important part of project management, especially at the end of a project. It helps to build morale, increase motivation, and create a positive culture within the team.

Conversely, failure to recognise and celebrate, achievement can result in disillusioned team members who feel that their efforts have not been seen or appreciated.

There are many ways to celebrate achievements and give team recognition, such as hosting a team party, giving out certificates or awards, or publicly acknowledging individual contributions. Some teams may also choose to create a team scrapbook or photo album to capture memories and highlight the project's successes.

A very small example of a project I ran where we did this was a series of 4 workshops I created and ran for the Royal Photographic Society titled "Street photography – get out and do it" in early 2023. At the end of the workshop series, I created a website in CANVA to showcase the work of the participants who wanted to put their work up – this was a lovely way to celebrate the efforts and talents of the participants and was appreciated by them as a public showcase of their abilities. The website can be seen at https://joehoughton.my.canva.site/rps-street-mar23

Whatever method is chosen, it's important to involve the entire team in the celebration and make sure everyone feels valued for their contributions.

Remember to keep the tone positive and emphasize the team's successes, rather than focusing on areas that need improvement.

Celebrating achievements is a great way to close out a project on a high note and set the stage for future success.

10.7.1 The Sales Conference - Closure

Closing down a project like a sales conference means tying off lots of loose ends. It's easier when you use an external venue like a conference centre as they do a lot of the physical stuff for you, but there will still be many things that cropped up over the event that need closing off properly.

Speakers may need to be paid, and other suppliers as well. Final tallies of what was spent must be made so they can be reconciled against the budget and a report compiled for the management team. Prizes may need shipping to those who couldn't attend the event in person.

A lessons learned event where you bring the event team together for a final review is an important but often overlooked part of the process.

Benefits of collating and storing lessons learned into some kind of corporate archive, are:

1 - that everybody is learnings and insights are actually captured, because, without a lessons learned event, these learning is very often stay in the heads of those who learned them, but go no further.

2 - the lessons learned become available for future teams. This retains organisational knowledge and turns tacit knowledge into explicit knowledge that can be reused in future. We may have found that a supplier let us down, or didn't do a very good job, and the lessons learned might flag up that that supplier shouldn't be used in future. We may have discovered a fabulous new speaker who would add value to future company events, so that would go down as well. Insights into the fact that launching five new products at the sales conference was actually too much for everybody to take on board at once might lead to future conferences becoming more effective.

It's often a good time after the lessons learned event to schedule the celebration party where the hard work and effort of the team who organised and run the event is recognised in some kind of a social gathering.

11 Key Project Management organisations

As with any major discipline, there are many organisations that can help you move forward in developing skills, networking with like-minded professionals and learn about best practices. This section lists some of the main project management organisations that you can join or access to further your knowledge of project management.

Here are five compelling reasons why you should consider becoming a member of a professional project management association:

1. **Networking opportunities**: One of the main advantages of joining a professional project management association is the opportunity to network with like-minded individuals in the industry. These connections can help you learn from experienced professionals, discover new job opportunities, and form lasting relationships that can support your career growth. Networking events organized by these associations can be invaluable in expanding your professional circle.

2. **Access to educational resources**: Professional project management associations often provide their members with a wealth of educational resources, such as webinars, workshops, conferences, and publications. These resources can help you deepen your understanding of project management principles, stay up-to-date with industry trends, and develop new skills. As a beginner, having access to these resources can significantly accelerate your learning process.

3. **Professional development opportunities**: By joining a project management association, you'll have access to various professional development opportunities, such as certification programs and specialized training courses. These programs can help you acquire new skills and demonstrate your competence in project

management, ultimately making you more attractive to potential employers and boosting your career prospects.

4. **Mentorship and support**: Many professional project management associations offer mentorship programs that can connect you with experienced project managers willing to share their knowledge and expertise. As a beginner, having a mentor can be invaluable in guiding you through the challenges of project management and helping you learn from real-world experiences. Additionally, these associations often provide support in the form of discussion forums, where you can ask questions and receive advice from fellow members.

5. **Enhancing your credibility**: Membership in a reputable project management association can add credibility to your professional profile. Employers and clients often view association membership as an indicator of your commitment to the profession and your dedication to staying current with industry best practices. By joining a professional project management association, you're signalling that you take your career seriously and are actively working to improve your skills and knowledge.

11.1 Prince2

Website: https://www.prince2.com/

PRINCE2 (PRojects IN Controlled Environments) is a widely recognized and practiced project management methodology. It is a process-based method that provides a structured approach to managing projects effectively. Originally developed as a UK Government standard, PRINCE2 has since gained popularity in the private sector, both in the UK and internationally.

The PRINCE2 methodology is designed to be adaptable and can be tailored to suit the specific needs of a project, regardless of its size or complexity. It focuses on key principles, themes, and processes that help guide project managers through each stage of a project, ensuring that it remains on track and delivers the intended outcomes.

Key principles of PRINCE2 include:

1. **Continued business justification**: Ensuring that a project remains viable and relevant throughout its duration.

2. **Learn from experience**: Applying lessons learned from previous projects to improve future project outcomes.

3. **Defined roles and responsibilities**: Clearly establishing the roles and responsibilities of each team member.

4. **Manage by stages**: Breaking the project down into manageable stages with regular progress reviews.

5. **Manage by exception**: Empowering project managers to make decisions within predefined boundaries, escalating issues only when necessary.

6. **Focus on products**: Concentrating on the delivery of quality outputs, rather than simply completing tasks.

7. **Tailor to suit the project environment**: Adapting the PRINCE2 methodology to fit the specific needs and constraints of each project.

PRINCE2's themes and processes help project managers apply these principles effectively throughout the project life cycle. The themes include aspects such as business case, organization, quality, plans, risk, change, and progress. The processes outline the key activities to be performed at each stage of the project, from initiation to closure.

For beginners in project management, PRINCE2 offers a comprehensive and structured approach that can help them manage projects more effectively. By learning and applying the PRINCE2 methodology, new project managers can build a strong foundation in project management principles and practices that can be adapted to suit a wide range of project environments.

11.2 The PMI

Website: https://www.pmi.org/

The Project Management Institute (PMI) is a globally recognized organization that promotes best practices and standards in project management. PMI offers resources, certifications, and a comprehensive framework for managing projects based on the Project Management Body of Knowledge (PMBOK).

The PMBOK is a set of guidelines and best practices that provides a standardized approach to project management. It outlines processes, tools, and techniques that can be applied to various projects across different industries. The PMBOK is organized into five main process groups, which coincide with the project management lifecycle:

1. **Initiating**: Defining the project scope, identifying stakeholders, and establishing objectives.

2. **Planning**: Developing a comprehensive project plan, including schedules, budgets, and resources.

3. **Executing**: Implementing the project plan and managing the project team to complete the work.

4. **Monitoring and controlling**: Tracking progress, managing risks, and making adjustments as needed to keep the project on track.

5. **Closing**: Finalizing project deliverables, conducting a post-project review, and celebrating achievements.

For beginners in project management, the PMI methodology and PMBOK provide a valuable framework that can help them understand and navigate the complexities of managing projects. By following the PMBOK guidelines, new project managers can develop their skills and knowledge in a structured and standardized way.

PMI offers various levels of certification to validate a project manager's competency in applying the PMBOK principles and practices. Two of the most popular certifications are:

1. **Certified Associate in Project Management** (CAPM): This entry-level certification is designed for individuals who are new to project management or those looking to gain a foundational understanding of project management principles. To obtain the CAPM certification, candidates must pass an exam covering the knowledge areas outlined in the PMBOK.

2. **Project Management Professional** (PMP): The PMP certification is an advanced credential for experienced project managers who have demonstrated proficiency in applying the PMBOK principles and practices. To be eligible for the PMP certification, candidates must meet specific education and experience requirements and pass a rigorous exam.

In summary, the PMI organization and its methodology offer a solid foundation for beginning project managers. By studying the PMBOK and pursuing PMI certifications such as CAPM and PMP, new project managers can enhance their skills, knowledge, and credibility in the field of project management.

Project Management made easy...

11.3 The APM

Website: https://www.apm.org.uk/

The Association for Project Management (APM) is a reputable organisation that focuses on advancing the field of project management. APM offers resources, professional development, and certifications to help project managers develop their skills and knowledge.

The APM framework is a methodology that provides a structured approach to project management, making it suitable for beginners. The APM framework consists of five interconnected phases:

1. **Envision**: This phase corresponds with the Initiation phase in the PMBOK. In the Envision phase, a project is conceptualized, and all stakeholders are identified. The possible objectives of the project, along with potential risks and constraints, are also explored. This phase is crucial for setting the foundation of the project and ensuring that all parties have a clear understanding of what the project entails.

2. **Speculate**: During the Speculate phase, the project team works on developing a detailed project plan, including the project scope, timeline, and resources required. This phase involves brainstorming and refining ideas to ensure that the project is feasible and aligns with the organisation's goals and objectives.

3. **Explore**: In the Explore phase, the project team begins executing the project plan. The focus is on actively managing risks, monitoring progress, and adjusting the plan as necessary to address any emerging issues or changes in scope. Effective communication and collaboration among team members are crucial during this phase.

4. **Adapt**: The Adapt phase involves reviewing the project's progress and performance, identifying areas for improvement, and making

adjustments to the plan to ensure the project stays on track. This phase may involve revising the project scope, reallocating resources, or adjusting the timeline to account for unforeseen challenges.

5. **Close**: The final phase in the APM framework is the Close phase. In this phase, the project team finalizes deliverables, conducts a post-project review, and documents lessons learned. The project's success is evaluated, and the team celebrates the achievements.

For beginning project managers, the APM organisation and its methodology offer a practical and structured approach to project management. By following the APM framework, new project managers can build their skills and knowledge while managing projects effectively. APM also offers various certifications and professional development opportunities to help project managers further enhance their skills and credibility in the field of project management.

11.4 Agile Alliance

Website: https://www.agilealliance.org/

The Agile Alliance is an organization that promotes the use of Agile methodologies in project management. Agile methodologies emphasize iterative development, collaboration, and adaptability, making them an excellent choice for managing projects in fast-paced and dynamic environments. As a beginner in project management, you can benefit from understanding the Agile approach and how it can be applied to various projects.

Agile project management focuses on breaking projects down into smaller, manageable phases called sprints. Each sprint has a specific duration, usually between 2 to 4 weeks, during which the team works on completing a subset of tasks or features. At the end of each sprint, the team reviews the work done, gathers feedback from stakeholders, and adjusts the project plan as needed. This iterative approach allows for continuous improvement and adaptation to changing requirements or unforeseen challenges.

There are several Agile frameworks that you can consider for your projects, including:

1. **Scrum**: Scrum is a popular Agile framework that uses time-boxed sprints and well-defined roles (such as the Scrum Master, Product Owner, and Development Team) to facilitate communication, collaboration, and rapid delivery of high-quality products. Scrum also utilizes regular meetings, like daily stand-ups, sprint reviews, and sprint planning sessions, to keep the team aligned and focused on the project goals.

2. **Kanban**: Kanban is another Agile framework that emphasizes visualizing the project's workflow, limiting work in progress (WIP), and continuously improving processes. A Kanban board is used to represent the project's tasks, which are moved through different

stages (e.g., To Do, In Progress, and Done) as they are completed. This approach helps teams identify bottlenecks and optimize their workflow for efficiency.

3. **Extreme Programming (XP)**: XP is an Agile framework that focuses on software development projects. It emphasizes high-quality code, frequent releases, and continuous integration. XP incorporates practices like test-driven development, pair programming, and continuous refactoring to ensure the best possible outcomes.

As a beginner in project management, the Agile Alliance and its methodologies can provide you with valuable insights and tools to manage projects effectively in dynamic and uncertain environments. By adopting Agile principles, you can build a collaborative and adaptable project management approach that delivers better results and increased customer satisfaction.

11.5 Scrum Alliance

Website: https://www.scrumalliance.org/

The Scrum Alliance is a non-profit organization that promotes the use of Scrum, an Agile framework, in project management. The organization offers training, certification, and resources to help professionals and organizations adopt and implement Scrum effectively. As a beginner in project management, understanding the Scrum Alliance and its methodology can provide you with valuable insights and tools for managing projects more efficiently and delivering better results.

The Scrum methodology is based on iterative development, close collaboration between team members, and continuous improvement. It divides projects into smaller, time-boxed phases called sprints, usually lasting between two to four weeks. During each sprint, the team focuses on completing a set of prioritized tasks or features that contribute to the project's overall goals.

Some key elements of the Scrum framework include:

1. **Scrum roles**: There are three main roles in Scrum - the Scrum Master, the Product Owner, and the Development Team. The Scrum Master facilitates the Scrum process, removes obstacles, and ensures the team follows Scrum principles. The Product Owner is responsible for defining the project's requirements, prioritizing tasks, and ensuring that the team delivers value to stakeholders. The Development Team works together to complete tasks and deliver high-quality results.

2. **Scrum events**: Scrum has several important events or meetings that facilitate communication, collaboration, and continuous improvement. These include the Daily Stand-up, Sprint Planning, Sprint Review, and Sprint Retrospective. Each event serves a specific purpose, such as coordinating team efforts, planning the next sprint, or reflecting on past performance to improve future work.

3. **Scrum artifacts**: The Scrum framework uses several artifacts to visualize and track the project's progress.

    - The **Product Backlog** is a prioritized list of features or tasks that the team needs to complete.

    - The **Sprint Backlog** contains the tasks selected for the current sprint.

    - The **Increment** is the working product or result produced at the end of each sprint.

As a beginner in project management, the Scrum Alliance can provide valuable resources and support for adopting Scrum in your projects. By understanding and implementing the Scrum framework, you can create a more collaborative, adaptable, and efficient project management approach that helps your team deliver better results and increase customer satisfaction.

11.6 IPMA – International Project Management Association

Website: https://www.ipma.world/

The International Project Management Association (IPMA) is a global non-profit organization that focuses on promoting project management best practices, competence development, and certification. IPMA is dedicated to advancing the project management profession and helping professionals improve their skills and abilities.

The IPMA methodology is based on the Individual Competence Baseline (ICB), a comprehensive manual that outlines 29 competence elements essential for a successful project manager. These competence elements are grouped into three main categories:

1. **Technical competences**: These competences cover various aspects of project management, such as scope, time, cost, quality, risk, and procurement. As a beginner, you'll need to understand the basics of these technical aspects and how they impact your project's success.

2. **Behavioural competences**: These competences focus on the interpersonal skills and personal attributes needed for effective project management. They include leadership, communication, teamwork, and conflict resolution. Developing these skills will help you work more effectively with your team and stakeholders.

3. **Contextual competences**: These competences are related to the broader organizational and environmental context in which the project takes place. They include understanding the project's strategic alignment, governance structures, and legal and regulatory requirements. As a project manager, you'll need to navigate these contextual factors to ensure your project's success.

IPMA offers a four-level certification scheme based on the ICB competence elements:

1. Level D (Certified Project Management Associate): Suitable for beginners, this certification demonstrates a fundamental understanding of project management concepts and practices.

2. Level C (Certified Project Manager): Aimed at professionals with some experience in managing projects, this certification requires proven competence in managing non-complex projects.

3. Level B (Certified Senior Project Manager): This certification is for experienced project managers who have demonstrated the ability to manage complex projects.

4. Level A (Certified Projects Director): The highest level of certification, aimed at professionals who have demonstrated competence in managing multiple complex projects or programs.

As a beginner in project management, familiarizing yourself with the IPMA methodology and competence elements can provide a solid foundation for developing your skills and advancing your career. By pursuing the appropriate level of certification, you can demonstrate your commitment to professional growth and gain recognition for your project management expertise.

11.7 IPM – Institute of Project Management

Website: https://www.projectmanagement.ie/

The Institute of Project Management (IPM) was established in 1989 as the first Irish professional body dedicated to promoting project management. With over 40,000 professionals trained, IPM is globally recognized as the leading Irish education and certification authority providing project management courses.

While the IPM does not have its own unique project management methodology, it does offer training and certification programs that align with globally recognized project management methodologies and frameworks such as PMI's PMBOK, PRINCE2, Agile, and Scrum.

For beginning project managers, IPM provides courses that help build a solid foundation in project management concepts and best practices. The organization's training courses cover various aspects of project management, including project initiation, planning, execution, monitoring, control, and closure. These courses also emphasize key skills, such as effective communication, stakeholder management, risk management, and team management.

11.8 LCI - Lean Construction Institute

Website: https://leanconstruction.org/

The Lean Construction Institute (LCI) is an organization whose mission is to transform the design and build environment by reforming production management in design, engineering, and construction for capital facilities. LCI has developed the Lean Project Delivery System™ (LPDS), which applies lean principles pioneered in manufacturing to the construction industry.

For beginning project managers, understanding the Lean Construction Institute's methodology can provide valuable insights into efficient project management, particularly within the construction sector. The core focus of the LPDS is to reduce waste, enhance value, and improve overall project outcomes. This is achieved through continuous improvement, collaboration, and the elimination of inefficiencies.

The main components of the Lean Project Delivery System™ include:

1. **Project definition**: Clearly defining project objectives, scope, and success criteria.

2. **Lean design**: Ensuring the design process maximizes value and minimizes waste through collaboration, innovative problem-solving, and the use of efficient design tools.

3. **Lean supply**: Streamlining the procurement and delivery of materials and services to minimize waste and ensure timely availability.

4. **Lean assembly**: Implementing efficient construction processes, promoting collaboration among team members, and using prefabrication and modular construction techniques to reduce waste and improve project performance.

5. **Use and maintenance**: Incorporating lifecycle considerations into project planning, focusing on long-term sustainability, and reducing the environmental impact of the project.

For beginners in project management, embracing the Lean Construction Institute's methodology can help improve project performance, reduce waste, and promote collaboration among team members. By applying lean principles to construction projects, project managers can optimize resources, enhance value, and deliver successful projects more efficiently.

12 Project Management Methodologies

Project management methodologies refer to the various approaches used to plan, execute, and control projects. These methodologies provide a framework for managing projects and ensure that they are completed on time, within budget, and to the satisfaction of stakeholders. In this section, we will provide a very brief overview of some of the most commonly used project management methodologies: Waterfall, AGILE, Six Sigma, Lean, Lean Six Sigma, and Total Quality Management (TQM). Each methodology is then explained in further detail below.

Waterfall

Waterfall is a traditional project management methodology that follows a sequential, linear approach. The methodology involves dividing the project into distinct phases, each of which must be completed before the next phase can begin. The phases typically include requirements gathering, design, development, testing, and deployment. Waterfall is best suited for projects with well-defined requirements and a clear understanding of the end product.

Agile

Agile is an iterative project management methodology that emphasizes flexibility and adaptability. The methodology involves dividing the project into small, manageable parts called sprints. Each sprint typically lasts two to four weeks and involves the completion of a set of deliverables. Agile is best suited for projects with rapidly changing requirements and a need for continuous feedback and iteration.

Six Sigma

Six Sigma is a data-driven project management methodology that focuses on reducing defects and improving quality. The methodology involves defining, measuring, analysing, improving, and controlling processes to achieve a desired level of quality. Six Sigma is best suited for projects with a focus on process improvement and quality control.

Lean

Lean is a project management methodology that focuses on minimizing waste and maximizing value. The methodology involves identifying and eliminating activities that do not add value to the project. Lean is best suited for projects with a focus on efficiency and waste reduction.

Lean Six Sigma

Lean Six Sigma combines the principles of Lean and Six Sigma to create a comprehensive project management methodology that focuses on minimizing waste, maximizing value, and improving quality. The methodology involves identifying and eliminating activities that do not add value to the project, while also using data-driven analysis to identify and eliminate defects and improve quality.

Total Quality Management (TQM)

TQM is a project management methodology that focuses on continuous improvement and customer satisfaction. The methodology involves a commitment to quality at all levels of the organization, from senior management to frontline workers. TQM is best suited for projects with a focus on customer satisfaction and continuous improvement.

12.1 Useful Resources

There are a variety of resources available for project managers looking to learn more about project management methodologies. Here are a few up-to-date resources that project managers may find useful:

1. Project Management Institute (PMI) - PMI is a professional association for project managers that offers a variety of resources, including training, certifications, and best practices for managing projects using different methodologies.

2. Agile Alliance - Agile Alliance is a non-profit organization that promotes Agile project management and offers a variety of resources, including training and events.

3. Six Sigma - The official Six Sigma website offers a variety of resources, including training, certification, and best practices for managing projects using Six Sigma.

4. Lean Enterprise Institute - The Lean Enterprise Institute offers a variety of resources, including training and events, for managing projects using Lean.

5. American Society for Quality (ASQ) - ASQ is a professional association for quality management professionals that offers a variety of resources, including training, certifications, and best practices for managing projects using TQM.

12.2 Waterfall

The waterfall methodology is one of the oldest and most widely used project management methodologies. It follows a linear, sequential approach to project management, with each phase of the project completed before moving on to the next phase. The methodology was originally developed in the manufacturing industry and was later adapted for use in software development and other project-based industries.

The stages of the waterfall methodology typically include requirements gathering, design, development, testing, and deployment. Each phase must be completed before moving on to the next, and changes to requirements or design are generally not allowed once the project has moved past the requirements gathering phase. This makes the waterfall methodology best suited for projects with well-defined requirements and a clear understanding of the end product.

One of the main advantages of the waterfall methodology is that it provides a clear framework for project management, with each phase clearly defined and structured. This can make it easier to manage projects and ensure that they are completed on time and within budget. However, the rigid structure of the waterfall methodology can also be a disadvantage, as it can make it difficult to accommodate changes in requirements or design during the project lifecycle.

There are a variety of resources available for project managers looking to learn more about the waterfall methodology and how it can be best used. Here are a few up-to-date resources that project managers may find useful:

The Project Manager website offers a comprehensive overview of the methodology, including its history, stages, and best practices. It can be found at https://www.projectmanager.com/guides/waterfall-methodology .

In conclusion, the waterfall methodology is a well-established and widely used project management methodology that can be effective for projects with well-defined requirements and a clear understanding of the end product.

However, its rigidity can make it less suitable for projects with rapidly changing requirements or a need for continuous feedback and iteration. By understanding the strengths and weaknesses of different project management methodologies and selecting the one that best fits the project requirements, project managers can increase the chances of project success.

12.3 Agile

Agile project management is a flexible and iterative approach to project management that has gained popularity in recent years. It originated in the software development industry as a response to the shortcomings of traditional project management methodologies, such as the waterfall methodology.

12.3.1 History and Development of Agile

The Agile methodology was first introduced in 2001 in the Agile Manifesto, a set of guiding principles for software development. The manifesto was developed by a group of software developers who were dissatisfied with the rigid and inflexible nature of traditional project management methodologies.

The Agile Manifesto emphasized the importance of individuals and interactions, working software, customer collaboration, and responding to change. The principles laid out in the manifesto were based on the belief that software development is an iterative and collaborative process that requires flexibility and adaptability.

Since the introduction of the Agile Manifesto, Agile methodology has evolved and expanded to other industries beyond software development. Today, Agile project management is used in a wide range of industries, including construction, manufacturing, and marketing.

12.3.2 How Agile Differs from Waterfall

The Agile methodology differs from traditional project management methodologies, such as the waterfall methodology, in several key ways.

1. **Flexibility and Adaptability**

Agile project management is more flexible and adaptable than traditional project management methodologies. Instead of following a rigid, linear approach, Agile projects are divided into small, manageable parts called sprints. Each sprint focuses on completing a set of deliverables, and feedback is continuously incorporated into the development process.

2. Collaboration and Communication

Agile project management emphasizes collaboration and communication among team members and stakeholders. This helps to ensure that everyone is working towards the same goals and that feedback is incorporated into the project as it progresses.

3. Customer Satisfaction

Agile project management places a strong emphasis on customer satisfaction. By continuously incorporating feedback from customers and stakeholders, Agile projects can be tailored to meet their specific needs and requirements.

4. Time and Cost Management

Agile project management focuses on managing time and costs through the use of sprints and continuous feedback. This allows project managers to identify and address issues early on, reducing the risk of delays and cost overruns.

12.3.3 Why Agile is Better than Waterfall for Modern Projects

Agile project management is better than the waterfall methodology for many modern projects because of its flexibility, adaptability, and focus on customer satisfaction. In today's fast-paced business environment, projects often require quick turnaround times and the ability to respond to changing requirements. Agile project management allows for this flexibility, enabling projects to be completed quickly and efficiently.

Additionally, Agile project management emphasizes collaboration and communication, which is essential for modern projects that require input and feedback from multiple stakeholders. This ensures that everyone is working towards the same goals and that projects are completed to the satisfaction of stakeholders.

There are many resources on Agile project management. Here are a few that new users of the Agile methodology might find useful:

1. **Agile Alliance** - Agile Alliance is a non-profit organization that promotes Agile project management and offers a variety of resources, including training, events, and a community forum. Their website is at https://www.agilealliance.org/ .

2. **Scrum Alliance** - Scrum Alliance is a non-profit organization that provides resources, training, and certification for Agile project management using the Scrum framework. Their website is at https://www.scrumalliance.org/ .

12.3.4 An AGILE Glossary of terms

Here's a glossary of key terms used throughout the AGILE methodology:

Term	Description
Acceptance Criteria	A set of predefined requirements that a product or feature must meet in order to be considered complete and accepted by stakeholders.
Agile	A project management and product development approach that emphasizes flexibility, collaboration, and customer satisfaction. Agile methods are iterative, allowing for frequent adjustments and improvements throughout the project lifecycle.
Agile Manifesto	A document outlining the key principles and values of Agile development, created in 2001 by a group of software developers. The Agile Manifesto prioritizes individuals and interactions, working solutions, customer collaboration, and responding to change.
Backlog	A prioritized list of tasks, features, or requirements that need to be addressed during the project lifecycle. The backlog is continually updated and refined as the project progresses.
Backlog Grooming	The process of reviewing, refining, and prioritizing items in the product backlog. This can include adding, updating, or removing tasks and features to ensure the backlog remains current and focused on delivering value.
Burndown Chart	A visual representation of the work remaining in a sprint, showing the progress made and estimating when the sprint will be completed. It helps teams identify whether they are on track to complete the work within the allotted time.

Term	Description
Burnup Chart	A visual representation of the work completed over time, showing the progress made and the total scope of the project. This can help teams understand how their work contributes to the overall project progress.
Continuous Integration	A development practice that involves regularly merging code changes into a shared repository, helping to detect and fix integration issues more quickly.
Continuous Deployment	A development practice that involves automatically deploying code changes to production after they have passed automated testing, reducing the time between development and release.
Cross-functional Team	A team composed of members with diverse skills and expertise, allowing them to work together to complete a project without relying on external resources. Cross-functional teams are a key component of Agile project management.
Daily Stand-up	A daily meeting where team members share their progress, plans, and any obstacles they face. The purpose is to keep everyone informed and to identify issues that may require assistance or further discussion.
Definition of Done	A shared understanding among team members about the criteria that must be met for a task or feature to be considered complete. This helps ensure that work is consistently and thoroughly completed across the team.
Epic	A large, complex work item that can be broken down into smaller tasks or user stories. Epics typically span multiple sprints or releases.

Term	Description
Feature	A specific functionality or capability that is part of a product or service. Features are typically developed in response to user needs or requirements.
Iteration	A short, fixed-length period of time during which a team works to complete a specific set of tasks or features. Iterations are a core component of Agile project management and are also known as sprints in Scrum.
Kanban	An Agile framework that emphasizes visualizing work, limiting work in progress, and optimizing the flow of tasks through various stages of completion. Kanban is often represented with a board that displays the status of tasks as they move through the workflow.
Lean-Agile	A combination of Lean and Agile principles and practices, focusing on minimizing waste, maximizing value, and delivering high-quality products in short, iterative cycles. Lean-Agile encourages continuous improvement and adaptation.
Minimum Viable Product (MVP)	A version of a product with just enough features to satisfy early customers and gather feedback for further development. MVPs are often used in Agile environments to quickly deliver value and iteratively improve the product based on user feedback.
Planning Poker	An estimation technique used by Agile teams to collaboratively estimate the effort required to complete tasks or user stories. Team members use a deck of cards with numerical values to represent their estimates, helping to reduce bias and promote discussion.

Term	Description
Product Owner	The person responsible for defining and prioritizing the product backlog, ensuring that the team is working on the most valuable tasks and features. The product owner represents the interests of the stakeholders and acts as the primary point of contact between the development team and the business.
Release	The process of making a product or feature available to customers, typically after it has been tested and approved by the development team and stakeholders. In Agile environments, releases are often smaller and more frequent, allowing for quicker feedback and adaptation.
Retrospective	A meeting held at the end of an iteration or sprint where the team reflects on their performance and identifies areas for improvement. Retrospectives are an important aspect of Agile project management, promoting continuous learning and growth.
Roadmap	A high-level, strategic plan that outlines the overall direction and goals of a project or product. Roadmaps provide a long-term view and help guide the team's priorities and decision-making. They are often updated and revised as the project progresses and new information becomes available.
Scrum	An Agile project management framework that emphasizes iterative development, collaboration, and transparency. Scrum uses fixed-length iterations called sprints, daily stand-up meetings, and a product backlog to help teams manage their work and deliver high-quality products.

Term	Description
Scrum Master	A facilitator and coach for an Agile team, responsible for ensuring that the team follows the Scrum process and continuously improves its practices. The Scrum Master removes obstacles, protects the team from external distractions, and helps to foster a collaborative and productive environment.
Sprint	A fixed-length iteration, typically lasting two to four weeks, during which an Agile team works to complete a specific set of tasks or features. Sprints are a core component of Scrum and other Agile methodologies.
Sprint Backlog	A subset of the product backlog that contains the tasks and features selected for the current sprint. The sprint backlog is owned by the development team and is used to track progress and plan their work during the sprint.
Sprint Goal	A short, high-level description of the desired outcome for a sprint, providing a focus and direction for the team. The sprint goal is agreed upon by the team and product owner at the beginning of the sprint and is used to guide the selection of items from the product backlog.
Sprint Planning	A meeting held at the beginning of a sprint where the team and product owner review the product backlog, select items for the sprint, and create a sprint backlog. The team also agrees on a sprint goal and estimates the effort required to complete the selected tasks.

Term	Description
Sprint Review	A meeting held at the end of a sprint where the team demonstrates the work completed during the sprint and gathers feedback from stakeholders. The sprint review helps to ensure that the work meets the requirements and provides an opportunity to adjust plans and priorities based on new information.
Story Points	A unit of measure used to estimate the effort or complexity of a task or user story in Agile project management. Story points help teams compare the relative size of tasks and allocate resources more effectively.
Task Board	A visual representation of the tasks and their progress within a sprint, often displayed as a physical or digital board with columns for different stages of completion. Task boards help teams track their work, identify bottlenecks, and communicate their status to stakeholders.
Timeboxing	A technique used in Agile project management to allocate a fixed amount of time for a specific activity, such as a sprint or a meeting. Timeboxing helps to maintain focus, increase productivity, and prevent tasks from taking longer than expected.
User Story	A concise, informal description of a feature or requirement from the perspective of an end-user. User stories are written in a format that emphasizes the user's needs and the value they will gain from the feature, helping to guide the development process and ensure that the product meets the users' expectations. User stories often follow the format: "As a [user role], I want to [action or goal], so that [benefit or value]."

Term	Description
Velocity	A metric used to measure the amount of work completed by an Agile team during a sprint or iteration. Velocity is typically measured in story points or the number of tasks completed and can be used to estimate how much work the team can realistically achieve in future sprints.
WIP (Work in Progress) Limit	A constraint on the number of tasks that can be in progress at any given time in a specific stage of the workflow. WIP limits are commonly used in Kanban and other Agile methodologies to prevent bottlenecks, maintain a steady flow of work, and encourage the team to focus on completing tasks before starting new ones.
Workflow	The sequence of steps or stages that a task must pass through from initiation to completion. In Agile project management, workflows are often visualized using task boards or Kanban boards, helping teams track their progress and identify bottlenecks.
XP (eXtreme Programming)	An Agile software development methodology that emphasizes rapid development, frequent releases, and continuous improvement. XP incorporates practices such as pair programming, test-driven development, and continuous integration to improve software quality and responsiveness to changing requirements.
Zero Bug Policy	A practice in Agile project management where teams prioritize fixing existing bugs before implementing new features or enhancements. The goal is to minimize technical debt and maintain a high level of software quality.

12.4 Six Sigma

Six Sigma is a project management methodology that aims to reduce defects and improve quality by identifying and eliminating variation in processes. It was developed by Motorola in the mid-1980s as a response to the company's need for a more effective way to improve quality and reduce defects.

The key components of Six Sigma are encapsulated in the acronym DMAIC, and include:

1. **Define**: The first step in the Six Sigma process is to define the problem and the goals of the project. This includes identifying the process to be improved and setting clear, measurable goals.

2. **Measure**: The second step is to measure the process to identify where defects and variation are occurring. This includes collecting data on the process and analysing it to identify areas of improvement.

3. **Analyse**: The third step is to analyse the data to determine the root cause of defects and variation. This includes identifying factors that contribute to the problem and developing a hypothesis about how to address it.

4. **Improve**: The fourth step is to implement changes to the process to address the root cause of defects and variation. This includes testing and validating the changes to ensure that they are effective.

5. **Control**: The final step is to control the process to ensure that the changes are sustained over time. This includes monitoring the process to ensure that it continues to meet the goals of the project.

Six Sigma has become a widely used methodology in many industries, including manufacturing, healthcare, and finance. It has been shown to be effective in reducing defects, improving quality, and increasing efficiency.

12.4.1   DMADV - a variant of the DMAIC approach

The DMADV approach is a variant of the Six Sigma methodology that is used for new product development. It stands for Define, Measure, Analyse, Design, and Verify.

The main difference between DMADV and DMAIC is that DMAIC is used to improve existing processes, while DMADV is used to develop new products. DMAIC focuses on identifying and reducing variation in existing processes, while DMADV focuses on designing new products that meet customer needs and specifications.

Here is a brief overview of each step in the DMADV approach:

1. **Define**: In the Define phase, the project goals and objectives are established, and the voice of the customer is captured to identify customer requirements and preferences.

2. **Measure**: In the Measure phase, the team collects and analyses data on the customer requirements and other key factors that will impact the development of the new product.

3. **Analyse**: In the Analyse phase, the team analyses the data to identify the key drivers of customer satisfaction and to determine the critical-to-quality characteristics that will be used to guide the design of the new product.

4. **Design**: In the Design phase, the team uses the critical-to-quality characteristics to develop a detailed design of the new product. This phase involves testing and refining the design to ensure that it meets customer requirements and specifications.

5. **Verify**: In the Verify phase, the team validates the new product design through testing and customer feedback. This phase ensures

that the product is ready for production and meets all customer requirements and specifications.

The DMADV approach is particularly useful for new product development because it emphasizes the importance of understanding customer needs and preferences, and designing products that meet those needs. It also ensures that products are designed with a focus on quality and efficiency, reducing the risk of defects and other issues that can impact customer satisfaction.

In conclusion, the DMADV approach is a variant of the Six Sigma methodology that is used for new product development. It is similar to the DMAIC approach used for process improvement, but it is focused specifically on designing new products that meet customer needs and specifications. The DMADV approach emphasizes the importance of understanding customer requirements and preferences, and designing products that meet those needs while also ensuring quality and efficiency.

12.4.2 Six Sigma resources

Here are some external materials :

12.4.2.1 iSix Sigma

iSixSigma is a comprehensive resource for Six Sigma information, offering a variety of articles, forums, and tools for implementing Six Sigma projects. The website is at https://www.isixsigma.com/ .

12.4.2.2 ASQ

The American Society for Quality (ASQ) is a professional association that offers training, certification, and resources for implementing Six Sigma projects. Their website is at https://asq.org/ .

12.4.2.3 Six Sigma for Dummies

Six Sigma for Dummies is a book by Craig Gygi, Bruce Williams, and Terry Gustafson that provides a practical introduction to Six Sigma methodology for beginners. Amazon link - https://amzn.to/3IZcwLw .

12.4.3 A Six Sigma Glossary of terms

Term	Description
Affinity Diagram	A visual tool used to organize and prioritize ideas, issues, or data by grouping them based on their relationships or similarities.
Black Belt	A Six Sigma professional with advanced knowledge and experience in Six Sigma methodologies, responsible for leading project teams and implementing process improvements.
Cause-and-Effect Diagram	Also known as the Ishikawa or fishbone diagram, it is a graphical tool used to identify, explore, and display the possible causes of a particular problem or variation in a process.
Control Chart	A statistical tool used to monitor process performance over time by plotting data points against established control limits, enabling the identification of trends, shifts, or other variations in the process.
Control Phase	The final phase of the Six Sigma DMAIC process, where the improved process is monitored, and control mechanisms are put in place to ensure the process remains stable and improvements are sustained.
Control Plan	A detailed document outlining the steps, procedures, and monitoring processes required to maintain control and ensure the process continues to meet the desired performance levels.

CTQ	Critical to Quality, a characteristic or attribute of a product or service that directly impacts its ability to meet customer requirements or expectations.
DMAIC	An acronym for Define, Measure, Analyse, Improve, and Control; it is the structured problem-solving methodology used in Six Sigma projects to improve existing processes.

Term	Description
DMADV	An acronym for Define, Measure, Analyse, Design, and Verify; it is the Six Sigma methodology used for designing new products, services, or processes to meet customer requirements and expectations.
FMEA	Failure Modes and Effects Analysis, a systematic and proactive technique used to identify, prioritize, and mitigate potential failure modes and their causes in a process, product, or system.
Green Belt	A Six Sigma professional with intermediate knowledge and experience in Six Sigma methodologies, responsible for supporting Black Belts in project execution and leading smaller projects.
Histogram	A graphical representation of data distribution by grouping data points into specified intervals or "bins," providing insights into the shape, spread, and central tendency of the data. Also known as a bell shaped curve.
Kaizen	A Japanese term meaning "continuous improvement," referring to the practice of making small, incremental improvements to processes or systems on an ongoing basis.
KPI	Key Performance Indicator, a measurable value that indicates how well a process, system, or organization is performing in relation to its strategic goals or objectives.
Lean	A systematic approach to identify and eliminate waste and non-value-added activities from processes, focusing on maximizing customer value with minimal resources.
Master Black Belt (MBB)	A Six Sigma professional with the highest level of expertise and experience in Six Sigma methodologies, responsible for training, coaching, and mentoring other Six Sigma practitioners, and driving the strategic deployment of Six Sigma within an organization.

Term	Description
Pareto Chart	A type of bar chart that displays the frequency or impact of problems, issues, or defects, arranged in descending order, used to identify and prioritize the most significant factors contributing to a problem. Based on the Pareto Principle, which states that 80% of the effects come from 20% of the causes.
Poka-Yoke	A Japanese term meaning "error-proofing," referring to a technique used to prevent mistakes

12.5 LEAN

LEAN is a project management methodology that emphasizes the elimination of waste and the optimization of processes. It originated in the manufacturing industry in Japan, where it was used by Toyota to improve their manufacturing processes in the 1950s.

12.5.1 The key principles of LEAN

1. **Value**: The first principle of LEAN is to focus on delivering value to customers. This requires a deep understanding of customer needs and preferences, as well as a commitment to meeting those needs in the most efficient and effective way possible.

2. **Flow**: The second principle of LEAN is to ensure that work flows smoothly and efficiently through the system. This requires the elimination of bottlenecks, delays, and other obstacles that can impede the flow of work.

3. **Pull**: The third principle of LEAN is to create a system in which work is pulled through the system by customer demand. This requires a deep understanding of customer needs and preferences, as well as a commitment to delivering value to customers in the most efficient and effective way possible.

4. **Perfection**: The final principle of LEAN is to continuously strive for perfection by eliminating waste and improving processes. This requires a commitment to continuous improvement and a willingness to challenge existing assumptions and practices.

12.5.2 Stages of LEAN project development

1. **Define Value**: The first stage of LEAN project development is to define value from the perspective of the customer. This requires a deep understanding of customer needs and preferences, as well as a commitment to meeting those needs in the most efficient and effective way possible.

2. **Map the Value Stream**: The second stage of LEAN project development is to map the value stream, which is the series of steps required to deliver value to the customer. This requires an understanding of the entire process, including all inputs, outputs, and activities.

3. **Create Flow**: The third stage of LEAN project development is to create flow by eliminating obstacles, bottlenecks, and other barriers to the efficient flow of work. This requires a commitment to continuous improvement and a willingness to challenge existing assumptions and practices.

4. **Establish Pull**: The fourth stage of LEAN project development is to establish pull by creating a system in which work is pulled through the system by customer demand. This requires a deep understanding of customer needs and preferences, as well as a commitment to delivering value to customers in the most efficient and effective way possible.

5. **Pursue Perfection**: The final stage of LEAN project development is to pursue perfection by continuously striving to eliminate waste and improve processes. This requires a commitment to continuous improvement and a willingness to challenge existing assumptions and practices.

12.5.3 The 7 types of waste

As a project management methodology , LEAN aims to eliminate waste and optimize processes. In order to achieve this goal, LEAN seeks to identify and eliminate the seven types of waste that can occur in any project or process. These seven types of waste are:

1. **Overproduction**: This occurs when more products or services are produced than are needed, leading to excess inventory and wasted resources.

2. **Waiting**: This occurs when people or processes are idle due to delays or bottlenecks, leading to wasted time and resources.

3. **Transport**: This occurs when products or materials are moved unnecessarily, leading to wasted time, energy, and resources.

4. **Inappropriate processing**: This occurs when processes are unnecessarily complex or involve unnecessary steps, leading to wasted time, energy, and resources.

5. **Excess inventory**: This occurs when more inventory is held than is needed, leading to wasted space, time, and resources.

6. **Unnecessary motion**: This occurs when people or equipment move unnecessarily, leading to wasted time, energy, and resources.

7. **Defects**: This occurs when products or services are not produced to the required standard, leading to wasted time, energy, and resources.

By identifying and eliminating these seven types of waste, LEAN can help to optimize processes and improve efficiency.

Here are some resources that can help you amplify your knowledge of LEAN:

12.5.4 Lean Enterprise Institute

The Lean Enterprise Institute is a non-profit organization that offers training, resources, and events related to LEAN management. Their website is at https://www.lean.org/ .

12.5.5 The Toyota Way

"*The Toyota Way*" is a book by Jeffrey Liker that describes the principles and practices of LEAN management as practiced by Toyota. Amazon link - https://amzn.to/41Ogqj3 .

12.5.6 The Lean Startup

"*The Lean Startup*" is a book by Eric Ries that describes how LEAN principles can be applied to startup companies to improve their chances of success. Amazon link - https://amzn.to/3Zt9syn .

12.5.7 LEAN Production

LEAN Production is a website that offers a variety of resources and tools related to LEAN manufacturing, including articles, webinars, and training courses. URL is https://www.leanproduction.com/ .

12.5.8 A LEAN glossary of terms

Term	Description
Acceptance Criteria	A set of predefined requirements that a product or feature must meet in order to be considered complete and accepted by stakeholders.
Agile	A project management and product development approach that emphasizes flexibility, collaboration, and customer satisfaction. Agile methods are iterative, allowing for frequent adjustments and improvements throughout the project lifecycle.
Agile Manifesto	A document outlining the key principles and values of Agile development, created in 2001 by a group of software developers. The Agile Manifesto prioritizes individuals and interactions, working solutions, customer collaboration, and responding to change.
Backlog	A prioritized list of tasks, features, or requirements that need to be addressed during the project lifecycle. The backlog is continually updated and refined as the project progresses.
Backlog Grooming	The process of reviewing, refining, and prioritizing items in the product backlog. This can include adding, updating, or removing tasks and features to ensure the backlog remains current and focused on delivering value.

Project Management made easy...

Term	Description
Burndown Chart	A visual representation of the work remaining in a sprint, showing the progress made and estimating when the sprint will be completed. It helps teams identify whether they are on track to complete the work within the allotted time.
Burnup Chart	A visual representation of the work completed over time, showing the progress made and the total scope of the project. This can help teams understand how their work contributes to the overall project progress.
Continuous Deployment	A development practice that involves automatically deploying code changes to production after they have passed automated testing, reducing the time between development and release.
Continuous Integration	A development practice that involves regularly merging code changes into a shared repository, helping to detect and fix integration issues more quickly.
Cross-functional Team	A team composed of members with diverse skills and expertise, allowing them to work together to complete a project without relying on external resources. Cross-functional teams are a key component of Agile project management.
Daily Stand-up	A daily meeting where team members share their progress, plans, and any obstacles they face. The purpose is to keep everyone informed and to identify issues that may require assistance or further discussion.

Term	Description
Definition of Done	A shared understanding among team members about the criteria that must be met for a task or feature to be considered complete. This helps ensure that work is consistently and thoroughly completed across the team.
Epic	A large, complex work item that can be broken down into smaller tasks or user stories. Epics typically span multiple sprints or releases.
Feature	A specific functionality or capability that is part of a product or service. Features are typically developed in response to user needs or requirements.
Iteration	A short, fixed-length period of time during which a team works to complete a specific set of tasks or features. Iterations are a core component of Agile project management and are also known as sprints in Scrum.
Kanban	An Agile framework that emphasizes visualizing work, limiting work in progress, and optimizing the flow of tasks through various stages of completion. Kanban is often represented with a board that displays the status of tasks as they move through the workflow.
Lean	A set of principles and practices aimed at minimizing waste and maximizing value in a process or system. Lean thinking is focused on delivering value to customers and eliminating activities that do not contribute to that value.

Term	Description
Lean-Agile	A combination of Lean and Agile principles and practices, focusing on minimizing waste, maximizing value, and delivering high-quality products in short, iterative cycles. Lean-Agile encourages continuous improvement and adaptation.
Milestone	A significant event or achievement in the project lifecycle that marks the completion of a phase or a set of tasks. Milestones are often used to measure progress and keep stakeholders informed.
Minimum Viable Product (MVP)	A version of a product with just enough features to satisfy early customers and gather feedback for further development. MVPs are often used in Agile environments to quickly deliver value and iteratively improve the product based on user feedback.
MoSCoW Method	A prioritization technique used to categorize project requirements into four groups: Must-haves, Should-haves, Could-haves, and Won't-haves. This helps teams focus on delivering the most important features first.
PERT (Program Evaluation and Review Technique)	A project management tool used to analyse, plan, and schedule complex projects by breaking them down into smaller tasks and estimating the time required to complete each task. PERT allows for the calculation of the critical path and helps identify potential bottlenecks in the project.
Planning Poker	An estimation technique used by Agile teams to collaboratively estimate the effort required to complete tasks or user stories. Team members use a deck of cards with numerical values to represent their estimates, helping to reduce bias and promote discussion.

Term	Description
PMBOK (Project Management Body of Knowledge)	A comprehensive guide published by the Project Management Institute (PMI) that outlines best practices, processes, and knowledge areas in project management. The PMBOK is widely recognized as a key resource for project managers and is the basis for the Project Management Professional (PMP) certification
Product Owner	The person responsible for defining and prioritizing the product backlog, ensuring that the team is working on the most valuable tasks and features. The product owner represents the interests of the stakeholders and acts as the primary point of contact between the development team and the business.
Release	The process of making a product or feature available to customers, typically after it has been tested and approved by the development team and stakeholders. In Agile environments, releases are often smaller and more frequent, allowing for quicker feedback and adaptation.
Retrospective	A meeting held at the end of an iteration or sprint where the team reflects on their performance and identifies areas for improvement. Retrospectives are an important aspect of Agile project management, promoting continuous learning and growth.
Roadmap	A high-level, strategic plan that outlines the overall direction and goals of a project or product. Roadmaps provide a long-term view and help guide the team's priorities and decision-making. They are often updated and revised as the project progresses and new information becomes available.

Term	Description
Scrum	An Agile project management framework that emphasizes iterative development, collaboration, and transparency. Scrum uses fixed-length iterations called sprints, daily stand-up meetings, and a product backlog to help teams manage their work and deliver high-quality products.
Scrum Master	A facilitator and coach for an Agile team, responsible for ensuring that the team follows the Scrum process and continuously improves its practices. The Scrum Master removes obstacles, protects the team from external distractions, and helps to foster a collaborative and productive environment.
Sprint	A fixed-length iteration, typically lasting two to four weeks, during which an Agile team works to complete a specific set of tasks or features. Sprints are a core component of Scrum and other Agile methodologies.
Sprint Backlog	A subset of the product backlog that contains the tasks and features selected for the current sprint. The sprint backlog is owned by the development team and is used to track progress and plan their work during the sprint.
Sprint Goal	A short, high-level description of the desired outcome for a sprint, providing a focus and direction for the team. The sprint goal is agreed upon by the team and product owner at the beginning of the sprint and is used to guide the selection of items from the product backlog.

Term	Description
Sprint Planning	A meeting held at the beginning of a sprint where the team and product owner review the product backlog, select items for the sprint, and create a sprint backlog. The team also agrees on a sprint goal and estimates the effort required to complete the selected tasks.
Sprint Review	A meeting held at the end of a sprint where the team demonstrates the work completed during the sprint and gathers feedback from stakeholders. The sprint review helps to ensure that the work meets the requirements and provides an opportunity to adjust plans and priorities based on new information.
Story Points	A unit of measure used to estimate the effort or complexity of a task or user story in Agile project management. Story points help teams compare the relative size of tasks and allocate resources more effectively.
Task Board	A visual representation of the tasks and their progress within a sprint, often displayed as a physical or digital board with columns for different stages of completion. Task boards help teams track their work, identify bottlenecks, and communicate their status to stakeholders.
Timeboxing	A technique used in Agile project management to allocate a fixed amount of time for a specific activity, such as a sprint or a meeting. Timeboxing helps to maintain focus, increase productivity, and prevent tasks from taking longer than expected.

Term	Description
User Story	A concise, informal description of a feature or requirement from the perspective of an end-user. User stories are written in a format that emphasizes the user's needs and the value they will gain from the feature, helping to guide the development process and ensure that the product meets the users' expectations. User stories often follow the format: "As a [user role], I want to [action or goal], so that [benefit or value]."
Velocity	A metric used to measure the amount of work completed by an Agile team during a sprint or iteration. Velocity is typically measured in story points or the number of tasks completed and can be used to estimate how much work the team can realistically achieve in future sprints.
WIP (Work in Progress) Limit	A constraint on the number of tasks that can be in progress at any given time in a specific stage of the workflow. WIP limits are commonly used in Kanban and other Agile methodologies to prevent bottlenecks, maintain a steady flow of work, and encourage the team to focus on completing tasks before starting new ones.
Workflow	The sequence of steps or stages that a task must pass through from initiation to completion. In Agile project management, workflows are often visualized using task boards or Kanban boards, helping teams track their progress and identify bottlenecks.

Term	Description
XP (eXtreme Programming)	An Agile software development methodology that emphasizes rapid development, frequent releases, and continuous improvement. XP incorporates practices such as pair programming, test-driven development, and continuous integration to improve software quality and responsiveness to changing requirements.
Zero Bug Policy	A practice in Agile project management where teams prioritize fixing existing bugs before implementing new features or enhancements. The goal is to minimize technical debt and maintain a high level of software quality.

12.6 Lean Six Sigma

Lean Six Sigma is a methodology that combines the principles of LEAN and Six Sigma to create a comprehensive framework for improving quality and efficiency. It was created in the 1990s as a way to address the limitations of both LEAN and Six Sigma on their own.

The key features of Lean Six Sigma include:

1. **Focus on customer needs**: Lean Six Sigma places a strong emphasis on understanding and meeting the needs of customers, as this is the ultimate goal of any project or process.

2. **Data-driven decision making**: Lean Six Sigma relies on data analysis to identify and address the root causes of problems, rather than relying on assumptions or guesswork.

3. **Continuous improvement**: Lean Six Sigma is a continuous improvement methodology, meaning that it is an ongoing process of identifying and eliminating waste and improving processes.

4. **Combining LEAN and Six Sigma**: Lean Six Sigma combines the waste elimination principles of LEAN with the data-driven problem-solving approach of Six Sigma, creating a powerful methodology for improving quality and efficiency.

The advantages of Lean Six Sigma include:

1. **Improved quality**: Lean Six Sigma can help to identify and eliminate defects, reducing the likelihood of errors or defects in products or services.

2. **Increased efficiency**: Lean Six Sigma can help to identify and eliminate waste, reducing the time and resources required to complete a project or process.

3. **Customer satisfaction**: By focusing on customer needs and delivering high-quality products or services, Lean Six Sigma can improve customer satisfaction and loyalty.

4. **Cost savings**: By eliminating waste and improving efficiency, Lean Six Sigma can help to reduce costs and increase profitability.

Here are some external references that can help you amplify your knowledge of Lean Six Sigma:

12.6.1 Lean Six Sigma Institute

The Lean Six Sigma Institute offers training, certification, and consulting services related to Lean Six Sigma methodology. Their website is at https://leansixsigmainstitute.org/ .

12.6.2 The Lean Six Sigma Pocket Toolbook

This book provides a quick reference guide to the tools and techniques of Lean Six Sigma. Amazon link - https://amzn.to/3F3g7XZ .

12.6.3 Lean Six Sigma for Dummies

This book provides a beginner-friendly introduction to Lean Six Sigma methodology. Amazon link - https://amzn.to/41PBpCf .

12.6.4 The Six Sigma Handbook

This book provides a comprehensive guide to the principles and practices of Six Sigma methodology, which is a key component of Lean Six Sigma. Amazon link - https://amzn.to/3YrPXoA .

12.7 KANBAN

Kanban is a methodology used in project management to manage and improve workflow processes. It originated in the manufacturing industry in Japan, where it was used to improve efficiency in production lines.

In Kanban, tasks are represented as cards, which are moved across a visual board as they progress through the project process. This allows team members to see at a glance what tasks are in progress, what has been completed, and what still needs to be done.

One of the key principles of Kanban is to limit the amount of work in progress (WIP) at any given time. This helps to prevent team members from becoming overwhelmed with too many tasks, which can lead to delays and errors.

Kanban has since been adopted in various industries, including software development, where it has become a popular methodology for managing agile projects. It's often used in combination with other project management methodologies, such as Scrum or Lean Six Sigma, to create hybrid approaches that are tailored to specific projects or teams.

12.7.1 Some useful KANBAN resources:

12.7.1.1 Kanbanize

Website: https://kanbanize.com/

A Kanban software tool that can help you manage your project and visualize your workflow. It provides features such as task management, time tracking, analytics, and more.

12.7.1.2 LeanKit / PlanView

Website: https://leankit.com/

Another Kanban software tool that offers customizable boards, real-time collaboration, and integration with other project management tools like Jira and Trello.

12.7.1.3 Kanban University

Website: https://edu.kanban.university/

An organization that provides training and certification in Kanban methodology. They offer courses for both beginners and experienced practitioners, as well as certification exams.

12.7.1.4 The Kanban Guide

Website: https://www.kanbanize.com/kanban-resources/getting-started/what-is-kanban/

A free online resource that provides an overview of Kanban methodology, as well as practical guidance on how to implement it in your project. It covers topics such as visualizing work, limiting work in progress, and managing flow.

12.7.1.5 Agile Alliance

Website: https://www.agilealliance.org/

An online community that provides resources and support for Agile and Lean methodologies, including Kanban. They offer articles, webinars, conferences, and other events that can help you learn more about Kanban and how to apply it in your project.

12.7.2 A KANBAN Glossary of terms :

Term	Description
Backlog	A prioritized list of tasks that need to be completed in a project.
Cycle Time	The time it takes for a task to move from start to finish.
Lead Time	The time it takes for a task to move from request to completion.
Pull System	A system in which tasks are pulled through the project process only when the resources are available, rather than being pushed through the system based on a predetermined schedule.
Kanban Board	A visual representation of a project's tasks and their progress.
Kaizen	Continuous improvement through small, incremental changes in processes and practices.
WIP (Work In Progress)	The number of tasks that are currently being worked on but are not yet completed.
Kanban	A methodology for managing and improving workflow processes, primarily used in software development and manufacturing.
Kanban Card	A physical or digital card that represents a task in the Kanban system.

Term	Description
Little's Law	A mathematical formula that describes the relationship between throughput, cycle time, and work in progress.
Swimlane	A way of organizing the Kanban board by dividing it into horizontal lanes that represent different stages of the project or different teams involved in the project.
Takt Time	The average amount of time it takes to complete one unit of work, often used to determine the capacity of a team or process.

13 Common Project Management Mistakes and How to Avoid Them

Project management is a crucial process for organizations to deliver projects on time and within the available resource constraints. However, not all projects succeed, and inexperienced project managers are more prone to project failure. In this section, we will discuss some of the most common causes of project failure, and then expand on some of these further.

1. One of the main causes of project failure is **poor planning**. Project planning is a critical process in which the project manager identifies the scope of work, the project timeline, available resources, and other key details required to deliver a successful project. However, inexperienced project managers may lack the skills and knowledge needed to effectively plan a project, leading to incomplete or inadequate plans.

2. Another common cause of project failure is **poor communication**. Effective communication is essential for any successful project, and inexperienced project managers may lack the necessary skills to communicate effectively with stakeholders, team members, and other project contributors. This can lead to misunderstandings, delays, and other issues that can derail a project.

3. **Lack of stakeholder involvement** is another common cause of project failure. Projects can fail if stakeholders are not involved in the project management process, leading to a lack of buy-in and support for the project. Inexperienced project managers may not know how to effectively involve stakeholders and may fail to solicit feedback and input from them, leading to project failure.

4. **Inadequate resource management** is also a common cause of project failure. Inexperienced project managers may lack the skills and knowledge to effectively manage resources, leading to resource over-allocation or under-allocation, which can impact the project's

success. This can also result in cost overruns or schedule delays, which can have a significant impact on the project's overall success.

5. Finally, a **lack of project management experience** is a common cause of project failure. Inexperienced project managers may not have the necessary skills, knowledge, or experience to effectively manage projects. They may be unfamiliar with project management tools, techniques, and best practices, which can lead to ineffective project management and project failure.

To avoid project failure, inexperienced project managers can take several steps to improve their project management skills and knowledge. They can invest time in learning about project management best practices and techniques, such as project planning, risk management, and stakeholder management. They can also seek out mentorship or guidance from more experienced project managers or take formal project management training courses.

Effective communication is critical in project management, and inexperienced project managers can benefit from developing strong communication skills. This includes not only verbal and written communication skills but also active listening skills, which are essential for understanding stakeholder needs and requirements.

Inexperienced project managers can also benefit from developing their resource management skills. This includes identifying available resources, allocating resources appropriately, and managing resource conflicts. Effective resource management can help ensure that projects are delivered on time and within budget.

13.1 Not Defining the Project Scope

One of the most important aspects of project management is defining the project scope. A clear project scope defines the boundaries of a project, including what it will and will not include. Failing to define the scope sufficiently or correctly at the start of a project will almost always lead to significant problems down the line.

The dangers of not defining scope sufficiently or correctly at the start of a project include:

1. **Scope Creep**: Without clear boundaries, it is easy for a project to grow beyond its original scope, resulting in increased costs, longer timelines, and a failure to deliver on the original objectives.

2. **Missed Deliverables**: A lack of clarity around the project scope can lead to confusion and misunderstandings about what is expected. This can result in missed deliverables or deliverables that do not meet stakeholder expectations.

3. **Unclear Requirements**: Without a clear definition of the project scope, it can be difficult to understand what requirements are necessary to achieve the project's objectives. This can lead to requirements being missed or misunderstood, resulting in a product or service that does not meet stakeholder needs.

4. **Unnecessary Work**: Failing to define the scope sufficiently can lead to unnecessary work being done, which wastes time and resources. Without clear boundaries, team members may work on tasks that do not contribute to the project's objectives, resulting in a lack of focus and reduced productivity.

5. **Increased Risk**: A lack of clarity around the project scope can increase the risk of project failure. Without clear boundaries, it is difficult to manage project risks effectively, resulting in unexpected problems that can derail the project.

To avoid these dangers, it is important to define the project scope clearly and explicitly at the start of a project. This should involve identifying the project objectives, stakeholders, deliverables, timelines, and budget. It is also important to communicate the project scope to all team members and stakeholders to ensure that everyone understands the boundaries of the project and what is expected.

13.2 Not Managing Stakeholder Expectations

Effective stakeholder management is critical to the success of any project. Stakeholders can have a significant impact on a project's outcomes, and their expectations must be managed effectively to ensure that the project delivers on its objectives. Failure to manage stakeholder expectations properly can lead to a range of problems that can derail a project.

The dangers of not managing stakeholder expectations properly include:

1. **Missed Objectives**: Stakeholders can have different expectations for a project, and failing to manage these expectations can result in missed objectives. This can lead to frustration, disappointment, and a lack of confidence in the project team.

2. **Scope Creep**: Stakeholders can request changes to the project scope, which can lead to scope creep. This can result in increased costs, longer timelines, and a failure to deliver on the original objectives.

3. **Delayed Decisions**: Stakeholders can delay decisions by requesting additional information or by not providing feedback promptly. This can result in delays and a lack of progress, which can be frustrating for the project team.

4. **Conflict**: Stakeholders can have conflicting priorities or interests, which can result in conflict. This can be challenging to manage and can lead to delays, reduced productivity, and a negative impact on team morale.

To avoid these dangers, it is important to manage stakeholder expectations effectively. Here are some solutions to these potential pitfalls:

1. **Communication**: Effective communication is critical to managing stakeholder expectations. It is important to establish clear communication channels and to keep stakeholders informed of project progress and any changes to the project scope.

2. **Expectation Management**: It is important to manage stakeholder expectations from the start of the project. This involves setting clear objectives and timelines, defining the project scope, and identifying any potential risks or challenges.

3. **Stakeholder Analysis**: It is important to conduct a stakeholder analysis to identify stakeholders, their interests, and their level of influence. This can help you understand how best to manage stakeholder expectations and how to address any potential conflicts.

4. **Change Management**: It is important to have a change management process in place to manage any requests for changes to the project scope. This process should involve evaluating the impact of any proposed changes and obtaining approval from relevant stakeholders before implementing any changes.

13.3 Poor Resource Planning

Effective resource management is crucial to the success of any project. The resources required for a project can include anything from personnel, equipment, materials, and budget. Poor resource management can lead to delays, increased costs, and an inability to achieve project goals.

The dangers of poor resource management include:

1. **Over-allocating Resources**: Allocating too many resources to a project can result in unnecessary expenses, leading to budget overruns. This can also cause delays as resources may be underutilized, leading to a lack of productivity.

2. **Under-allocating Resources**: Allocating too few resources to a project can lead to delays and missed deadlines, as the project team may not have the necessary resources to complete tasks on time. This can lead to increased costs and a failure to meet project objectives.

3. **Poor Resource Planning**: Poor planning can lead to a mismatch between the resources required for a project and the resources that are available. This can lead to a lack of productivity and delays as the project team may have to wait for additional resources to become available.

To avoid these dangers, it is important to manage resources effectively. Here are some ways to combat falling into these failures:

1. **Resource Allocation**: It is important to allocate resources effectively to ensure that they are used efficiently. This involves identifying the resources required for each task, determining the availability of resources, and allocating them based on the project schedule.

2. **Resource Forecasting**: It is important to forecast the resources required for a project in advance. This involves estimating the resources required for each task and identifying any potential constraints that may impact resource availability. This can help to ensure that the necessary resources are available when needed.

3. **Resource Levelling**: Resource levelling involves smoothing out resource allocation to ensure that resources are not over-allocated or under-allocated. This can help to ensure that resources are used efficiently and that tasks are completed on time.

4. **Risk Management**: Risk management involves identifying potential risks that may impact resource availability and developing strategies to mitigate these risks. This can help to ensure that resources are available when needed, even in the event of unexpected events.

13.4 Ineffective Communication

Effective communication is essential in any project management process. Poor communication can cause delays, rework, and, in some cases, project failure. Here are some dangers of ineffective communication in a project, followed by suggestions on how to avoid them.

One danger of ineffective communication is that **stakeholders may not have a clear understanding of the project's goals**, deliverables, or timelines. This lack of clarity can lead to misaligned expectations and misunderstandings among stakeholders. To avoid this, project managers should develop a communication plan that outlines how and when they will communicate project updates to stakeholders.

Another danger of ineffective communication is that **team members may not have access to the information they need** to complete their tasks. When this happens, team members may work on tasks that are no longer a priority, leading to delays and wasted resources. To prevent this, project managers should ensure that team members have access to project information and encourage them to ask questions if they are unsure about their tasks.

Poor communication can also cause **conflicts among team members**. When team members have different ideas about how to approach a task, conflicts can arise, leading to a breakdown in team collaboration. To avoid this, project managers should encourage open communication and promote a collaborative team culture.

Lastly, ineffective communication can cause **delays in the project schedule**. When team members do not communicate project status updates, it can be challenging for the project manager to identify potential issues and adjust the project schedule accordingly. To avoid delays, project managers should establish regular communication channels and encourage team members to provide frequent updates.

13.5 Lack of collaboration

Lack of collaboration is a common project management mistake that can significantly impact the success of a project. Ineffective collaboration can lead to miscommunication, confusion, and delays, ultimately affecting the project's outcome. In this section, we will discuss the importance of collaboration in project management and offer advice on using online software to collaborate more effectively across a project team.

When team members fail to collaborate effectively, it can result in several issues, including:

1. **Miscommunication**: Poor collaboration can lead to misunderstandings and confusion about project goals, expectations, and deadlines, causing delays and errors.

2. **Duplication of efforts**: Without proper collaboration, team members may unintentionally work on the same tasks or overlook critical tasks, wasting time and resources.

3. **Reduced team morale**: Ineffective collaboration can create frustration and a lack of trust among team members, ultimately affecting their motivation and productivity.

4. **Inability to adapt to changes**: Poor collaboration can make it difficult for the team to adapt to changes in project scope or requirements, leading to potential project failure.

To avoid the issues caused by poor collaboration, consider using online project management and collaboration tools to enhance communication and teamwork. Here are some tips for using online software effectively:

1. **Choose the right tool**: Select a collaboration tool that meets your team's needs and preferences. Popular options include Trello,

Asana, Slack, and Microsoft Teams. Consider factors such as ease of use, scalability, and integration with other tools your team may be using.

2. **Establish a clear communication plan**: Develop a communication plan that outlines how your team will use the collaboration tool. This should include guidelines for sharing updates, setting deadlines, and discussing issues.

3. **Encourage real-time communication**: Use features like instant messaging, video conferencing, and collaborative editing to facilitate real-time communication and collaboration among team members.

4. **Set up organized project workspaces**: Create dedicated workspaces or boards for each project, with clear categories, lists, or columns to help team members easily access and manage tasks.

5. **Assign tasks and track progress**: Use the collaboration tool to assign tasks to team members, set deadlines, and monitor progress. This promotes accountability and ensures that everyone is aware of their responsibilities.

6. **Share and store project documents**: Use the collaboration tool's file-sharing and storage features to centralize project documents, making them easily accessible to all team members.

7. **Train your team**: Ensure that all team members are familiar with the collaboration tool and its features. Offer training or resources to help them use the tool effectively.

8. **Review and adjust**: Regularly review your team's use of the collaboration tool and make adjustments as needed to improve communication and efficiency.

14 Leadership and Team Management

Leadership and team management are crucial components of project management. The success of a project depends not only on the skills and knowledge of individual team members, but also on how well they work together and are led.

The PMBOK, APM and Prince2 frameworks all emphasize the importance of strong project leadership and effective team management. This involves understanding the strengths and weaknesses of team members, and adapting your leadership style to best support their needs and maximize their potential.

Situational leadership is an approach often used in project management, where the leader adapts their style to the specific situation or task at hand. This means that leaders must be flexible and able to respond to changing circumstances, such as shifting project requirements or team member availability.

Effective team management also involves clear communication, setting expectations and goals, monitoring progress, and providing feedback and recognition for accomplishments. Team members must feel empowered and motivated to do their best work, which in turn leads to better project outcomes.

Overall, strong leadership and team management are essential for successful project management. By harnessing the diversity and unique strengths of team members, and adapting your leadership style to the situation, you can create a high-performing team and achieve project success.

14.1 ECCSR and Leadership

The first 2 steps of the ECCSR model in particular here are applicable when we start to discuss leadership and teamwork in projects.

Many projects are high-pressure situations, and leadership can be compromised and behaviours can stray outside of ethical boundaries quite quickly when pressures to achieve and perform are exerted.

Using frameworks such as ECCSR help teams and governance bodies to focus on the fundamental importance of integrity and ethical behaviour when making decisions and setting up norms for work in a project.

Project organizations are created by those within and overseeing the project, and the culture, expectations and acceptable modes of operation need to be discussed and explicitly outlined – it's one of the reasons we have a Team Charter document in many projects. This stuff doesn't "just happen" – you make it happen!

14.2 Leadership Styles

As a project manager, leadership is an essential skill to ensure that your team stays on track and reaches their goals. There are many different leadership styles, and it is important to understand the advantages and disadvantages of each. Here are three distinct leadership styles that are commonly used by effective project managers:

14.2.1 Transformational Leadership:

Transformational leadership is a style of leadership that focuses on inspiring positive change in team members. This approach is characterised by leaders who are energetic, enthusiastic, and passionate about the success of their team. They are actively involved in the process and committed to helping each member of the group achieve their goals. Transformational leadership can be particularly beneficial in project management for several reasons.

- **Inspiring a shared vision:** A transformational leader has the ability to create a compelling vision for the project and communicate it effectively to the team. By doing so, they inspire and motivate team members to work towards a common goal, fostering a sense of unity and purpose.

- **Encouraging personal growth:** Transformational leaders take an active interest in the personal and professional development of their team members. By understanding each person's strengths and weaknesses, they can provide tailored support and guidance to help them grow, ultimately leading to a more skilled and effective project team.

- **Boosting morale and engagement:** The energetic and enthusiastic nature of transformational leaders can be contagious. They often create a positive working environment that encourages creativity and innovation. This increased engagement can lead to higher productivity and a greater likelihood of project success.

- **Adapting to change:** Projects often involve uncertainty and change. A transformational leader is well-equipped to handle such situations, as they are focused on finding innovative solutions and adapting to new circumstances. This flexibility can help the project team navigate obstacles and keep the project on track.

- **Empowering team members:** Transformational leaders believe in the capabilities of their team members and empower them to make decisions and take ownership of their tasks. By doing so, they foster a sense of responsibility and accountability, which can lead to better project outcomes.

14.2.2   Situational Leadership

Situational leadership is a flexible and adaptable leadership style that takes into account the unique needs and skill levels of individual team members. This approach allows leaders to create a more comfortable working environment for their employees by tailoring their leadership style to match the specific requirements of each team member. In project management, situational leadership can be particularly useful in several ways.

Customised support: As projects often involve team members with diverse skills and experience levels, situational leadership enables project managers to provide tailored guidance and support to each individual, ensuring that their needs are met and that they can contribute effectively to the project.

Enhanced communication: By adapting their leadership style to suit the needs of each team member, project managers can foster open and effective communication, which is essential for collaboration and project success.

Flexibility and adaptability: Projects can change rapidly and may require team members to learn new skills or adapt to different situations. Situational leadership allows project managers to adjust their approach as needed to support their team through these changes, ensuring a smoother transition and a more efficient project execution.

While there are numerous authors who have written about situational leadership, some notable figures who have contributed significantly to this field are:

Paul Hersey and Ken Blanchard: They are the originators of "**The Situational Leadership® Model**", which has become a widely recognised framework for understanding and applying situational leadership. Their book, "**Management of Organizational Behavior**" (1969), introduces this model and provides a comprehensive explanation of the concept.

A website with more on this model is https://situational.com/situational-leadership/, and the Amazon link to this book is at https://amzn.to/3zLQ9Fe.

Ken Blanchard, Patricia Zigarmi, and Drea Zigarmi: These authors co-wrote the book "**Leadership and the One Minute Manager**" (1985). In this work, they expand upon the Situational Leadership® Model and provide practical guidance on how to apply the principles of situational leadership in various settings, including project management. Amazon link for this book is at https://amzn.to/3KUEnPz.

14.2.3 Servant Leadership

Servant leadership is a leadership style that focuses on the growth and well-being of the team members, prioritising their needs and helping them develop both professionally and personally. A servant leader seeks to empower and support their team, enabling them to reach their full potential. This leadership approach can be particularly relevant in project management for several reasons:

Empowerment and collaboration: Servant leaders create an environment that promotes collaboration and shared decision-making, ensuring that team members feel valued and are actively involved in the project. This can lead to increased motivation, commitment, and overall project success.

Focus on individual growth: By prioritising the personal and professional development of each team member, servant leaders can help their team acquire new skills and knowledge, which can enhance their ability to contribute effectively to the project.

Building strong relationships: Servant leadership emphasises the importance of building strong, trusting relationships within the team. This can improve communication and teamwork, which are essential for successful project execution.

Notable authors who have written about servant leadership include:

Robert K. Greenleaf: Greenleaf is widely recognised as the founder of the servant leadership concept. His book, "***Servant Leadership: A Journey into the Nature of Legitimate Power and Greatness***" (1977), explores the principles of servant leadership and provides a foundation for understanding this approach. Greenleaf's website URL is https://www.greenleaf.org/ and the 25th anniversary edition of the book is on Amazon at https://amzn.to/3ZT8rPy.

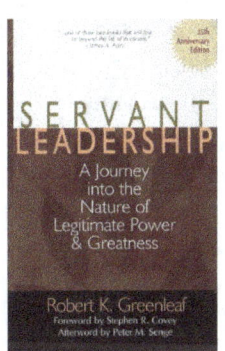

James C. Hunter: Hunter's book, "***The Servant: A Simple Story About the True Essence of Leadership***" (1998), is a popular work that presents servant leadership through a fictional narrative, making the concepts accessible and engaging for readers. Hunter's website URL is https://www.jameshunter.com/ and the Amazon link to the book is at https://amzn.to/40RjR7D.

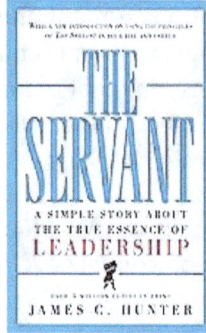

Larry C. Spears: Spears has edited and contributed to several books on servant leadership, including "***Reflections on Leadership: How Robert K. Greenleaf's Theory of Servant Leadership Influenced Today's Top Management Thinkers***" (1995). This book features essays from various authors discussing the impact of Greenleaf's work on modern leadership theories. Spears' website URL is https://www.spearscenter.org/ and the Amazon link to the book is at https://amzn.to/3KksLnj.

Each of these leadership styles can be effective, depending on the situation and the needs of the team. As a project manager, it's important to understand your team's strengths and weaknesses and adapt your leadership style to help them succeed. The PMI PMBOK, APM, and Prince2 frameworks all emphasize the importance of effective leadership in project management, so it's crucial to develop these skills if you want to excel in this field.

14.2.4 Core leadership styles - Lewin

Three core leadership styles - authoritarian, participative, and delegative - were identified by psychologist Kurt Lewin in the 1930's. Let's take a closer look at each of these styles and how they can be used in practical terms within project management.

1. **Authoritarian leadership**: This style involves a leader who maintains strict control over decision-making and often gives orders to subordinates. While this style can be effective in times of crisis or when decisions must be made quickly, it can also stifle creativity and discourage team members from contributing their own ideas. In project management, this style may be useful when a project is behind schedule or when a clear and decisive direction is needed.

2. **Participative leadership**: This style involves a leader who seeks input from team members and encourages collaboration. This style is often effective in fostering a positive team environment and can lead to greater buy-in from team members on project decisions. In project management, this style may be useful when working with a team of diverse backgrounds and skill sets, or when a project requires significant creativity or innovation.

3. **Delegative leadership**: This style involves a leader who delegates decision-making to subordinates and encourages them to take ownership of their work. While this style can be empowering for team members and allow for greater autonomy, it can also lead to confusion or inefficiency if team members are not properly trained or supported. In project management, this style may be useful when working with experienced team members who are skilled in their roles and can work independently.

It's important to remember that no one leadership style is inherently better than another - the most effective leaders are those who can adapt their style to meet the needs of their team and the project at hand. By being aware of your own natural leadership tendencies and open to feedback from team members, you can develop a leadership style that is effective and appropriate for the situation.

14.2.5 Leadership styles references

Mind Tools - Lewin's Leadership Styles Framework. Retrieved from https://www.mindtools.com/aieezpa/lewins-leadership-styles-framework

Project Management Institute. (2017). A Guide to the Project Management Body of Knowledge (PMBOK® Guide) (6th ed.). Project Management Institute.

14.3 Team Building

14.3.1 What is a team?

Do your people work in groups or teams? What's the difference?

The difference between a group and a team lies in the way they work together and how their work is assessed. In project management, it's essential to understand these differences to determine the best approach for your project.

A group consists of individuals who work in a shared space and have the same tasks, but each person is responsible for their own work. The members create separate pieces of work, which are then judged individually by managers. For example, in a software development project, a group of developers may be assigned to write code for various components. They work independently and submit their code to the project manager for evaluation.

On the other hand, a team is made up of members who collaborate to create a single, collective work or project. The team's performance is assessed as a whole, rather than by individual contributions. In project management, this approach is more aligned with the PMI, APM, and Prince2 frameworks, which emphasize collaboration, clear communication, and shared responsibility.

For example, consider a project where a team is tasked with designing a new website. The team might include a project manager, a designer, a developer, and a content writer. Instead of working on their own tasks separately, they collaborate closely to create a cohesive website. The project manager is responsible for overseeing the progress and ensuring that the team meets its objectives. The success of the project is determined by how well the team works together to achieve the desired outcome.

In summary, the main difference between a group and a team is the way they work together and how their work is assessed. A group consists of individuals working independently on separate tasks, while a team works collaboratively to create a single, collective work. In the context of project management, a team approach is often more effective, as it fosters collaboration, clear communication, and shared responsibility, which are key principles in PMI, APM, and Prince2 frameworks.

14.3.2 Building the team

Team building is an essential part of project management. Without it, a project team may not function cohesively, and this can lead to missed deadlines, miscommunications, and even project failure. Effective team building is about bringing together people with different backgrounds, skills, and perspectives and transforming them into a cohesive, high-performing team.

One practical way to achieve team cohesion is by creating opportunities for team members to get to know each other on a personal level. This can be done through social events, team-building exercises, and icebreaker activities. Another way is by encouraging open and honest communication, where team members feel comfortable expressing their opinions, sharing their ideas, and giving and receiving feedback.

In my university classes, where I teach project management and put the students into teams to complete projects, the first piece of homework that I always set them is to go to the pub. I tell them that they should go and not discuss the assignments that have been set, but instead spend the time getting to know each other.

Human beings are social animals, and making some specific time for group members to get to know each other, and start to understand the strengths, weaknesses, hopes and fears of those that they are working with helps turn people you don't know into colleagues that you can depend on and trust.

14.3.3 Tuckman's team formation cycle

The forming-storming-norming-performing cycle is a well-known model that describes the different stages a team goes through as it develops. The model was first introduced by Bruce Tuckman in 1965. According to Tuckman, the stages of team development include forming, storming, norming, and performing.

During the **forming** stage, team members are polite and friendly, and they focus on getting to know each other. During the **storming** stage, conflicts may arise as team members start to express their opinions and challenge each other's ideas. **Norming** is the stage where the team begins to resolve its conflicts and establish norms and expectations for behaviour. Finally, during the **performing** stage, the team is highly productive and cohesive.

Applying the forming-storming-norming-performing cycle to team building in project management means understanding that conflicts and disagreements are a natural part of the team development process. As a project manager, it's essential to create a safe and supportive environment for team members to express themselves, provide constructive feedback, and work collaboratively to achieve common goals. By doing this, you can help your team move through the different stages of team development and become a high-performing, cohesive unit.

This cycle was updated with Mary-Jane Jensen in 1977, when a fifth stage – adjourning was added, that looks at how to shut a project team down and disband it effectively.

14.3.4 Modern approaches to team building

Modern approaches to team building in project management have evolved to address the unique challenges and opportunities of the 21st century. These methods focus on fostering collaboration, problem-solving, adaptability, and innovation, making them particularly relevant for contemporary projects. Here are some key approaches and theories that are up-to-date and applicable in today's project management landscape:

1. **Problem-solving-based team building:** This approach involves an external consultant guiding the team through a series of exercises designed to help them identify and resolve issues. Typically conducted in a retreat setting, problem-solving-based team building encourages open communication, critical thinking, and collaboration, enabling teams to tackle challenges more effectively.

2. **Agile team building:** Inspired by the Agile project management methodology, this approach emphasises flexibility, adaptability, and iterative progress. Agile team building fosters a culture of continuous improvement, where team members regularly reflect on their performance, share feedback, and make adjustments to enhance their collaboration and overall project outcomes.

3. **Virtual team building:** With remote work becoming increasingly common in the 21st century, virtual team building has emerged as a critical component of project management. This approach incorporates online activities, games, and communication tools to help remote team members build trust, rapport, and a sense of camaraderie despite the physical distance between them.

4. **Strengths-based team building:** This approach focuses on identifying and leveraging the unique strengths of each team member. By understanding and capitalising on individual talents and skills, project managers can create more effective and balanced teams that are better equipped to handle diverse project challenges.

5. **Cross-functional team building:** This approach involves assembling a team composed of individuals from different departments,

backgrounds, and areas of expertise. Cross-functional team building encourages the exchange of diverse perspectives, fostering innovation and creative problem-solving that can lead to more successful project outcomes.

14.4 Conflict Management

Conflicts are an inevitable part of any project management process, no matter how well-planned or executed the project may be. Project managers need to be well-equipped to deal with conflicts in order to ensure the smooth running of the project. Conflict management involves identifying, addressing, and resolving conflicts in a way that maintains the integrity of the project and the relationships between team members.

It should be noted, however, that if conflict has been allowed to arise, it's often too late to make optimal use of the resources in the project. Good project managers apply proactive, and effective, inclusive communications to ensure that potential conflicts are identified, surfaced and addressed before they become bones of contention. Using a participative and consultative style, especially In the early stages of creating project plans can head off much conflict that otherwise will occur in later stages.

One practical method of conflict management is to establish clear communication channels. Encourage team members to express their concerns and provide them with opportunities to share their perspectives. Project managers should also be able to listen to all sides of the conflict and understand each team member's point of view. Another effective method is to encourage collaboration and compromise. Work with the team members to come up with creative solutions that address the needs of all parties involved.

The PMI, APM and Prince2 frameworks also provide guidance on conflict management. These frameworks suggest techniques such as negotiation, mediation, and arbitration to resolve conflicts. They also stress the importance of maintaining a positive working environment where team members can express their opinions and work together towards common goals.

14.5 Motivation

Motivation is the driving force that encourages individuals to take action towards achieving a goal. It is an essential part of a project manager's duties to ensure that team members remain motivated throughout the project's lifecycle. Without motivation, team members may lose interest in the project, become disengaged, and their productivity may decline.

A project manager can use various methods to motivate team members, such as setting clear expectations, providing regular feedback, recognizing and rewarding team members for their contributions, creating a positive work environment, and offering opportunities for growth and development. By keeping team members motivated, project managers can ensure that the project's objectives are met, and the project is delivered on time and within budget.

In addition, motivation plays a vital role in managing risks and resolving conflicts. Highly motivated team members are more likely to be engaged in finding solutions to issues, addressing risks proactively, and collaborating effectively with other team members. By fostering motivation within the project team, project managers can create a positive work culture and maintain high levels of team morale.

14.5.1 Points of view – the cathedral...

Simon Sinek recounts this wonderful story in his best-selling book *"Start with Why"*.

"Consider the story of two stonemasons. You walk up to the first stonemason and ask, "Do you like your job?" He looks up at you and replies, "I've been building this wall for as long as I can remember. The work is monotonous. I work in the scorching hot sun all day. The stones are heavy and lifting them day after day can be backbreaking. I'm not even sure if this project will be completed in my lifetime. But it's a job. It pays the bills." You thank him for his time and walk on.

About thirty feet away you walk up to a second stonemason. You ask him the same question, "Do you like your job?" He looks up and replies, "I love my job. I'm building a cathedral. Sure, I've been working on this wall for as long as I can remember and yes, the work is sometimes monotonous. I work in the scorching hot sun all day. The stones are heavy and lifting them day after day can be backbreaking. I'm not even sure if this project will be completed in my lifetime. But I'm building a cathedral"

Who do you want on your team? The first stonemason or the second one?

Motivating your team members is very often a matter of framing the situation for them. Get this right and they will see their job and what they are doing on the project in a far more positive way than just seeing it as a job to be done.

More on this story at https://digital-dream-lifestyle.com/2018/05/09/the-story-of-two-stonemasons/

15 Tools for Project Management

Project management software has become essential for running modern projects effectively, as it helps address various aspects of project management, such as cost, quality, communications, integration, time, scope, human resources, and risk management. These tools can streamline processes, improve collaboration, and provide better visibility into project progress. In this section, we'll briefly compare the following project management software and offer advice on which might be most suited for a beginner project manager: Microsoft Project, Microsoft Planner, Gantter, TeamGantt, OpenProject, ClickUp, Wrike, Monday.com, Trello, and Asana. More detailed explanations of each piece of software follows this section.

1. **Microsoft Project**: This is a powerful and flexible project management tool suitable for managing large or complex projects. It might be overwhelming for beginners, but its advanced features and integrations with other Microsoft 365 applications can be beneficial for more experienced project managers.

2. **Microsoft Planner**: Planner is a simpler, more user-friendly alternative to Microsoft Project. It is ideal for small to medium-sized projects and integrates well with other Microsoft 365 applications. Its visual, board-based interface makes it easy for beginners to track tasks and collaborate with team members.

3. **Gantter**: This tool is focused on Gantt chart-based project management, which helps visualize project schedules and dependencies. Gantter is suitable for beginners who want to learn the basics of project management using Gantt charts.

4. **TeamGantt**: Similar to Gantter, TeamGantt is a tool that specializes in Gantt chart-based project management. It offers an intuitive interface and real-time collaboration features, making it a good

option for beginners who want to focus on Gantt chart planning and tracking.

5. **OpenProject**: OpenProject is an open-source project management tool that provides a comprehensive set of features, including task management, time tracking, and reporting. It may have a steeper learning curve for beginners but offers a cost-effective solution for those who are willing to invest time in learning the platform.

6. **ClickUp**: ClickUp is a versatile project management tool with features like time tracking, task assignment, and goal tracking. Its user-friendly interface and customizable views make it a good choice for beginners who want a comprehensive tool with room to grow as their project management skills develop.

7. **Wrike**: Wrike is a flexible project management tool that offers a balance between simplicity and advanced features. It is suitable for beginners who need a comprehensive solution but also want the ability to scale up as their project management skills and needs evolve.

8. **Monday.com**: Monday.com is a visually appealing and user-friendly project management tool with a focus on collaboration and automation. Its customizable boards and integrations with popular tools make it an excellent choice for beginners looking to streamline their project management processes.

9. **Trello**: Trello is a popular, Kanban-based project management tool that is easy to use and ideal for beginners. Its simple, card-based interface and seamless integrations with other tools make it a great starting point for new project managers.

10. **Asana**: Asana is a user-friendly project management tool with a focus on task management and team collaboration. Its intuitive interface and integration with popular tools make it an excellent

choice for beginners who want to improve their project management skills.

In conclusion, the most suitable project management software for a beginner project manager will depend on their specific needs, preferences, and budget.

Microsoft Planner, Trello, and Asana are all user-friendly options with a focus on collaboration and ease of use, making them great choices for beginners. As a new project manager, you may want to start with one of these tools and gradually explore more advanced options as your project management skills and needs evolve.

15.1 Microsoft Project

Website: https://www.microsoft.com/en-ie/microsoft-365/project/project-management-software

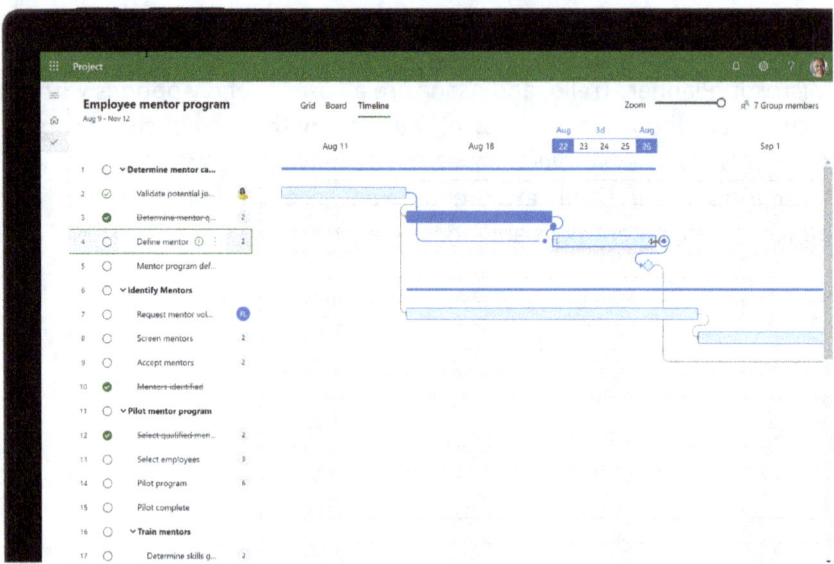

Probably the best known of all project management software, Microsoft Project is a powerful project management application designed to help businesses plan, manage, and deliver work effortlessly, from one-time projects to large initiatives. It offers a range of features that make it an effective tool for project management, aligning well with the principles of PMI, APM, and Prince2 frameworks.

However, it is relatively expensive and has quite a steep learning curve, so it would NOT be my recommendation for a beginner PM who is learning the ropes or trying out their skills on their first project.

Key reasons why Microsoft Project is an effective tool for project management include:

1. **Work flexibly**: Microsoft Project allows you to work with various project types, such as Waterfall, Agile, or a hybrid approach. This flexibility enables project managers to choose the methodology that best suits their project needs, aligning with the adaptability principle of PMI, APM, and Prince2 frameworks.

2. **Get visibility**: Microsoft Project provides a clear overview of project timelines, tasks, and resources, helping project managers track progress and identify potential bottlenecks. This visibility promotes effective monitoring and control, which are crucial aspects of project management frameworks.

3. **Plan projects**: The software allows you to create detailed project plans, including tasks, durations, dependencies, and resource allocations. This planning capability aligns with the PMI, APM, and Prince2 emphasis on thorough project planning and risk management.

4. **Share insights**: Microsoft Project enables easy sharing of project information with team members and stakeholders, fostering collaboration and clear communication. This feature supports the teamwork and stakeholder engagement principles present in PMI, APM, and Prince2 frameworks.

5. **Start quickly**: Microsoft Project offers a variety of pre-built templates and tools, allowing you to start managing your projects quickly and efficiently. This accessibility helps project managers focus on the critical aspects of their projects and aligns with the need for efficient project initiation in the PMI, APM, and Prince2 frameworks.

6. **Integration with other Microsoft tools**: Microsoft Project seamlessly integrates with other Microsoft 365 applications, such as Teams, Planner, and Power BI, which can enhance collaboration, communication, and reporting capabilities.

Project Management made easy...

15.2 Microsoft Planner

Website: https://tasks.office.com/

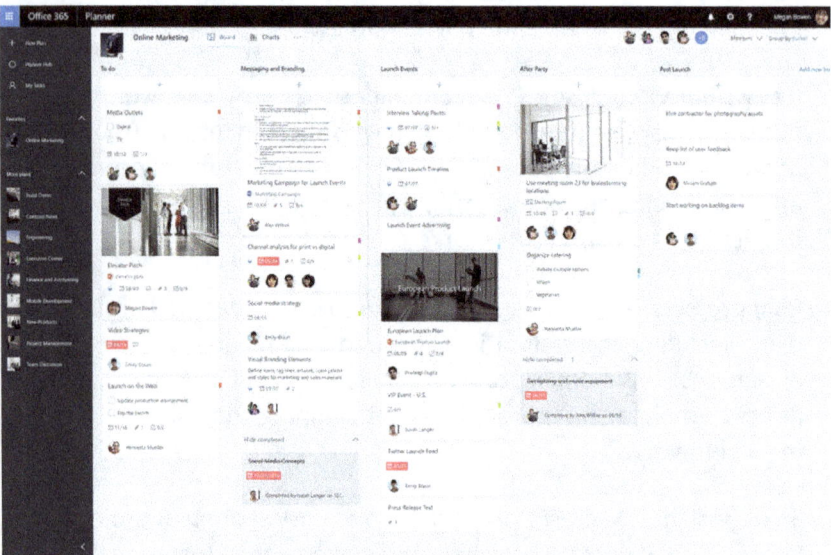

Microsoft Planner is an effective project management tool designed to help teams manage and monitor tasks in a shared plan. It offers a simple, user-friendly interface and is particularly suitable for small to medium-sized projects. Here are some reasons why Microsoft Planner is an effective project management tool:

1. **Visual task management**: Planner uses a board-based interface, allowing you to organize tasks into columns or "buckets" based on their status, priority, or any other custom categorization. This visual approach helps teams keep track of tasks and progress easily.

2. **Easy collaboration**: Microsoft Planner is designed to facilitate team collaboration. Team members can quickly create tasks, assign them to others, set due dates, and add attachments or notes. The tool also integrates seamlessly with other Microsoft 365 applications,

such as MS Teams, SharePoint, and Outlook, making it easy to collaborate and communicate within the context of your project.

3. **Task tracking and progress monitoring**: With Planner, you can set due dates for tasks and track their completion status. The tool also offers built-in charts and dashboards that provide an overview of the team's progress and help identify potential bottlenecks or delays.

4. **Customizable and flexible**: Planner allows you to customize your task boards to suit your team's needs. You can create custom labels for tasks, add checklists to break tasks into smaller steps, and filter tasks based on various criteria.

5. **Integration with Microsoft 365**: As part of the Microsoft 365 suite, Planner integrates seamlessly with other Microsoft applications, such as Teams for communication, SharePoint for document storage, and Outlook for calendar scheduling. This integration helps keep your team connected and ensures that all project-related information is easily accessible in one place.

As discussed in the previous section on page 270, Microsoft also offers a more advanced project management tool called Microsoft Project, which provides additional features and flexibility for managing larger or more complex projects. Microsoft plans to simplify and bring the experiences of Planner and Project closer together, making it easier for users to transition between the two tools as their project management needs evolve.

Project Management made easy...

15.3 Gannter

Website: https://www.gantter.com/

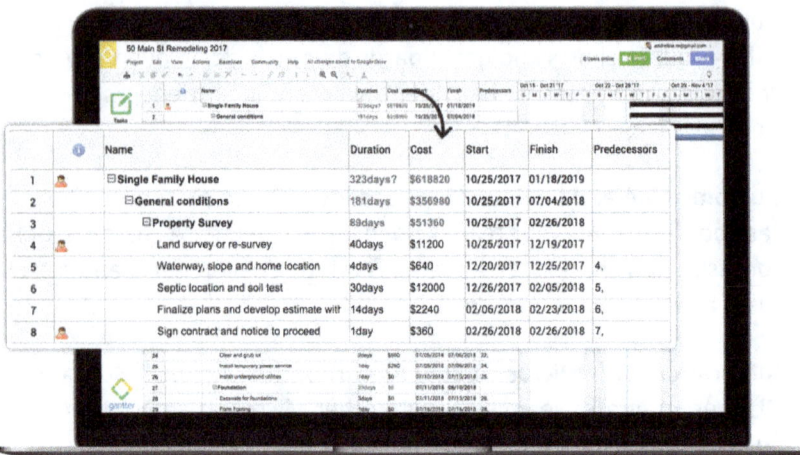

Gantt charts are a popular project management tool, and Gantter is a cloud-based software application that allows you to create and manage Gantt charts for your projects. Gantter is designed to help project managers plan, schedule, and visualize their projects effectively. It aligns with principles from the PMI, APM, and Prince2 frameworks, making it a valuable tool for project management.

Here's why Gantter is an effective project management tool:

1. **Visual representation**: Gantter provides a clear visual representation of your project schedule, with tasks displayed as horizontal bars spanning their duration. This helps project managers and team members quickly understand the project timeline, dependencies, and milestones, fostering better communication and coordination.

2. **Task management**: Gantter allows you to easily create, modify, and track tasks, including task start and finish dates, assignments of resources, priorities, and progress. This helps project managers

maintain control over their projects, in line with the PMI, APM, and Prince2 emphasis on effective task management.

3. **Resource management**: With Gantter, you can assign resources to tasks and monitor their utilization. This supports efficient resource allocation and management, which is a key aspect of the PMI, APM, and Prince2 frameworks.

4. **Collaboration**: Gantter is cloud-based, allowing team members to access and update project information in real-time from anywhere. This encourages collaboration and ensures that everyone is working with the most up-to-date information, aligning with the teamwork and communication principles present in PMI, APM, and Prince2 frameworks.

5. **Dependencies and critical path**: Gantter enables you to establish task dependencies, helping you identify and manage the critical path of your project. This feature supports effective project planning and risk management, which are central to the PMI, APM, and Prince2 methodologies.

6. **Integration with other tools**: Gantter can be integrated with popular project management and collaboration tools, such as Google Drive, Google Calendar, and Microsoft Project, which can enhance your project management capabilities and streamline your workflow.

Project Management made easy...

15.4 TeamGantt

Website: https://www.teamgantt.com/

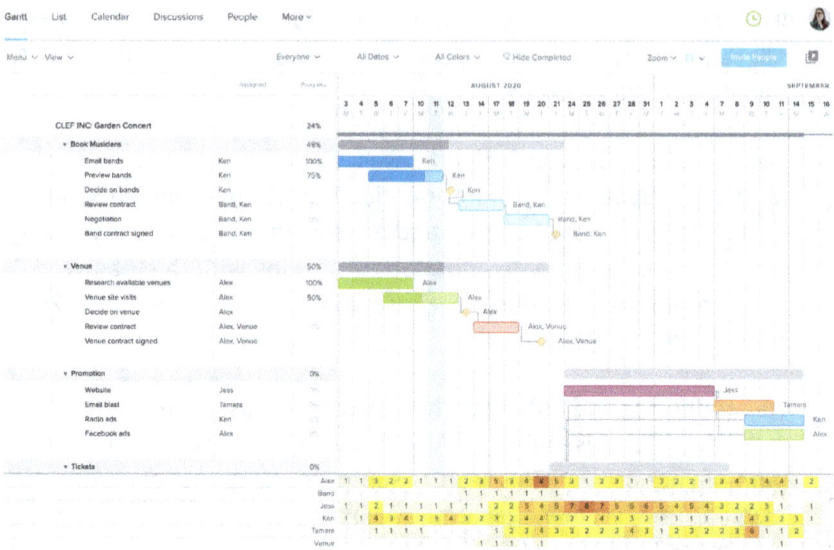

TeamGantt is a web-based project management tool that combines the power of Gantt charts with features designed to promote efficient teamwork and project execution. It aligns with the principles of the PMI, APM, and Prince2 frameworks, making it a valuable tool for project management.

Here are some reasons why TeamGantt is an effective project management tool:

1. **User-friendly Gantt charts**: TeamGantt allows you to create visually appealing and easy-to-understand Gantt charts that provide a clear overview of your project timeline, task dependencies, and milestones. This supports effective project planning and communication, in line with the PMI, APM, and Prince2 methodologies.

2. **Real-time collaboration**: TeamGantt's cloud-based platform enables team members to access, update, and collaborate on project information in real-time. This fosters teamwork, ensures up-to-date information, and aligns with the collaboration and communication principles of PMI, APM, and Prince2 frameworks.

3. **Progress tracking**: With TeamGantt, project managers can easily track task progress and see what's on time and what's running behind at a glance. This helps identify potential issues early and address them before they derail the project, which aligns with the monitoring and control aspects of PMI, APM, and Prince2 methodologies.

4. **Resource management**: TeamGantt allows you to assign tasks to team members and monitor their workload, promoting efficient resource allocation and management. This feature supports the resource management principles found in the PMI, APM, and Prince2 frameworks.

5. **Integration with other tools**: TeamGantt integrates with popular project management and collaboration tools, such as Slack, Trello, and Basecamp, which can enhance your project management capabilities and streamline your workflow.

6. **Customizable views and reporting**: TeamGantt offers customizable views, such as list view and calendar view, to suit different user preferences. Additionally, it provides project reporting features that help you analyse project performance and share insights with stakeholders, supporting the reporting and stakeholder engagement principles of the PMI, APM, and Prince2 frameworks.

Project Management made easy...

15.5 OpenProject

Website: https://www.openproject.org/

OpenProject (not to be confused with OpenProj, an older, discontinued project management software) is a versatile, open-source project management software designed to help teams effectively plan, execute, and monitor their projects. It offers a wide range of features that align with the principles of the PMI, APM, and Prince2 frameworks, making it an effective project management tool.

Here are some reasons why OpenProject is an effective project management tool:

1. **Project portfolio management**: OpenProject provides tools for managing multiple projects simultaneously, such as project lists, hierarchies, overviews, dashboards, and reports. This enables teams to effectively manage their project portfolio, in line with the portfolio management principles of the PMI, APM, and Prince2 frameworks.

2. **Project templates**: OpenProject allows users to create project templates to standardize projects and avoid starting from scratch. This feature ensures consistency across projects and saves time, aligning with the efficient project initiation and planning aspects of PMI, APM, and Prince2 methodologies.

3. **Collaboration**: OpenProject's cloud-based platform enables real-time collaboration among team members, fostering teamwork and clear communication. This supports the collaboration and communication principles present in the PMI, APM, and Prince2 frameworks.

4. **Task management**: OpenProject offers task management capabilities, including task creation, assignment, prioritization, and progress tracking. This supports effective project execution and control, which are essential aspects of PMI, APM, and Prince2 methodologies.

5. **Time and resource management**: OpenProject allows you to track time spent on tasks and monitor resource utilization, promoting efficient resource allocation and management. This aligns with the resource management principles of the PMI, APM, and Prince2 frameworks.

6. **Customizable views and reporting**: OpenProject provides customizable views, such as Gantt charts, Kanban boards, and calendar views, to suit different user preferences and project management methodologies. It also offers reporting features to help you analyse project performance and share insights with stakeholders, supporting the reporting and stakeholder engagement principles of the PMI, APM, and Prince2 frameworks.

7. **Open-source and scalability**: As an open-source software, OpenProject provides flexibility and scalability, allowing you to customize the tool according to your organization's specific needs and requirements.

15.6 ClickUp

Website: https://clickup.com/

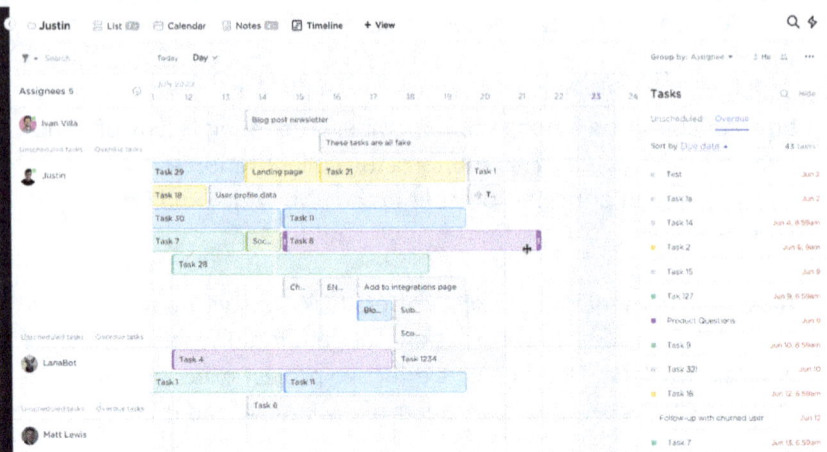

ClickUp is a comprehensive project management tool that offers a wide range of features to help teams manage and organize projects efficiently. It aligns with the principles of the PMI, APM, and Prince2 frameworks, making it an effective tool for project management.

Here are some reasons why ClickUp is an effective project management tool:

1. **Task management**: ClickUp allows you to create, assign, prioritize, and track tasks easily. This supports effective project execution and control, which are crucial aspects of the PMI, APM, and Prince2 methodologies.

2. **Time tracking**: ClickUp includes built-in time tracking features that enable you to monitor how much time is spent on tasks and assess team productivity. This promotes efficient resource allocation and management.

3. **Goal tracking**: With ClickUp, you can track your progress towards project goals, helping you identify bottlenecks earlier and prevent delays. This aligns with the monitoring and control aspects of PMI, APM, and Prince2 methodologies, ensuring project success.

4. **Customizable views**: ClickUp offers various customizable views, such as list view, board view, and Gantt chart view, to suit different user preferences and project management methodologies. This flexibility supports efficient project planning and communication.

5. **Real-time collaboration**: ClickUp's cloud-based platform enables real-time collaboration among team members, fostering teamwork and clear communication. This supports the collaboration and communication principles present in the PMI, APM, and Prince2 frameworks.

6. **Integration with other tools**: ClickUp integrates with popular project management and collaboration tools, such as Slack, Google Drive, and Trello, which can enhance your project management capabilities and streamline your workflow.

7. **Reporting and analytics**: ClickUp offers robust reporting and analytics features that help you analyse project performance, identify trends, and share insights with stakeholders.

Project Management made easy...

15.7 Wrike

Website: https://www.wrike.com/

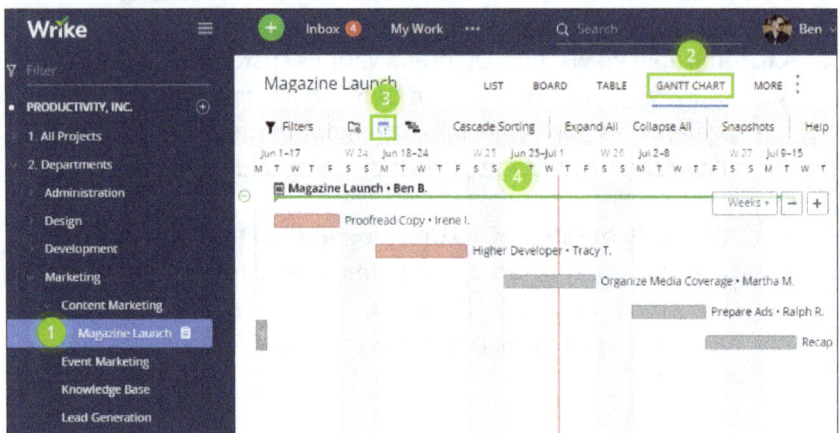

Wrike is a powerful and versatile project management software designed to help teams effectively estimate, plan, track, deliver, and bill for their services

Here are some reasons why Wrike is an effective project management tool:

1. **Comprehensive project planning**: Wrike enables you to create detailed project plans, set milestones, and establish dependencies, which supports effective project planning and execution.

2. **Task management**: Wrike allows you to create, assign, and prioritize tasks, as well as set deadlines and monitor progress. This helps ensure efficient project execution and control, crucial aspects of the PMI, APM, and Prince2 frameworks.

3. **Real-time collaboration**: Wrike's cloud-based platform enables real-time collaboration among team members, fostering teamwork and clear communication.

4. **Customizable views and dashboards**: Wrike offers various customizable views, such as list view, board view, and Gantt chart view, to suit different user preferences and project management methodologies. The customizable dashboards provide a clear overview of project progress.

5. **Time tracking and resource management**: Wrike includes built-in time tracking features and resource management capabilities that enable you to monitor how much time is spent on tasks and assess team productivity. This promotes efficient resource allocation and management.

6. **Integration with other tools**: Wrike integrates with popular project management and collaboration tools, such as Slack, Google Drive, and Microsoft Teams, which can enhance your project management capabilities and streamline your workflow.

7. **Reporting and analytics**: Wrike offers robust reporting and analytics features that help you analyse project performance, identify trends, and share insights with stakeholders.

15.8 Monday.com

Website: https://monday.com/

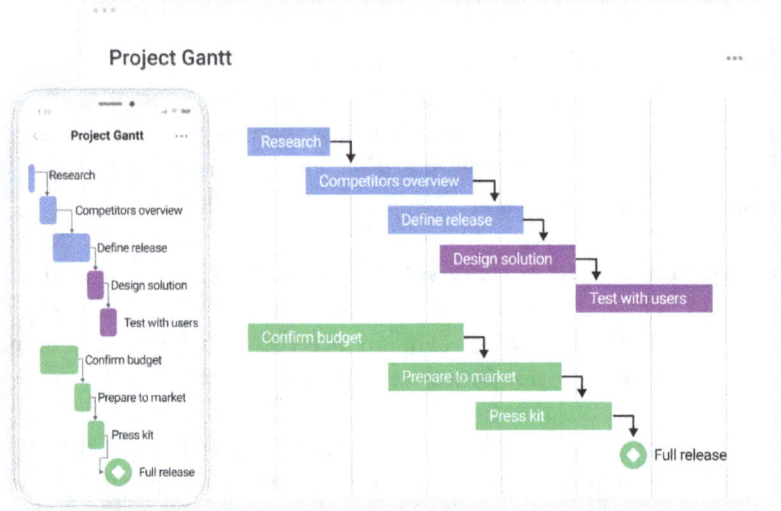

A relatively new entrant to the market, Monday.com is a popular and user-friendly project management tool designed to help teams collaborate, organize, and streamline their work processes. It offers various features that make project management more efficient compared to traditional methods, making it an effective choice for managing projects.

Here are some reasons why Monday.com is an effective project management tool:

1. **Intuitive interface**: Monday.com boasts an intuitive interface that makes it easy for users to create, manage, and visualize tasks and projects. Its simple drag-and-drop functionality makes it accessible for users with varying levels of technical expertise.

Project Management made easy...

2. **Customizable views**: Monday.com offers various customizable views, such as list view, board view, and calendar view, which cater to different user preferences and project management methodologies. This flexibility supports efficient project planning and communication.

3. **Real-time collaboration**: The platform enables real-time collaboration among team members, fostering teamwork and clear communication. With Monday.com, team members can easily share updates, leave comments, and attach files, ensuring everyone stays on the same page.

4. **Task management**: Monday.com allows you to create, assign, and prioritize tasks, set deadlines, and track progress. This helps ensure efficient project execution and control, which are crucial aspects of effective project management.

5. **Time tracking and resource management**: Monday.com includes time tracking features that enable you to monitor how much time is spent on tasks and assess team productivity. This promotes efficient resource allocation and management.

6. **Follow-up, evaluation, and feedback**: Monday.com makes it easier for project managers to follow up with team members, evaluate progress, and provide feedback. This continuous monitoring and evaluation help keep projects on track and improve overall performance.

7. **Integration with other tools**: Monday.com integrates with popular project management and collaboration tools, such as Slack, Google Drive, and Microsoft Teams, which can enhance your project management capabilities and streamline your workflow.

8. **Reporting and analytics**: Monday.com offers reporting and analytics features that help you analyse project performance, identify trends,

and share insights with stakeholders. This supports data-driven decision-making and ensures project success.

15.9 Trello

Website: https://trello.com/

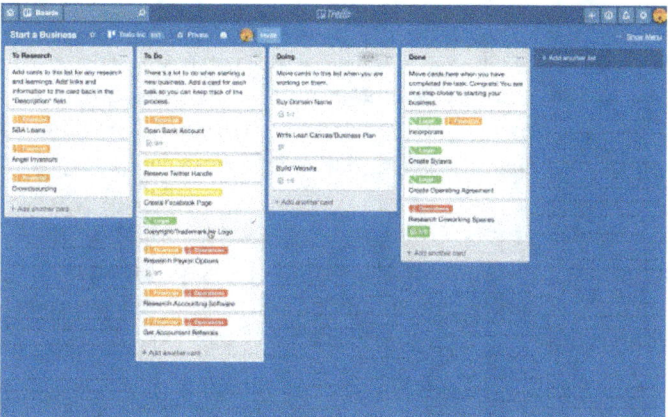

Trello is a user-friendly and visually appealing project management tool developed by Atlassian, which also offers a suite of tools like Jira, Confluence, and Team Central for project management, work management, and collaboration. Trello is based on the principles of a Kanban board, using cards and columns to track progress, making it an effective and efficient tool for managing projects. Here are some reasons why Trello is an effective project management tool:

1. **Visual layout**: Trello's Kanban board approach makes it easy for teams to visualize tasks and project progress. Cards represent tasks, and columns represent different stages of the project, making it easy to track and manage work as it moves through the process.

2. **Real-time collaboration**: Trello enables real-time collaboration among team members, fostering teamwork and clear communication. Team members can comment on cards, add attachments, and mention colleagues to ensure everyone is on the same page.

3. **Task management**: Trello allows you to create, assign, and prioritize tasks using cards. You can add due dates, labels, checklists, and custom fields to cards, ensuring efficient project execution and control.

4. **Flexible organization**: Trello's boards, lists, and cards can be customized to suit your project management needs. You can use Trello for various purposes, such as managing workloads, tracking project progress, organizing ideas, and more.

5. **Integration with other tools**: Trello integrates with popular project management and collaboration tools, such as Slack, Google Drive, and Microsoft Teams, which can enhance your project management capabilities and streamline your workflow.

6. **Notifications and reminders**: Trello's notification system keeps team members informed about important updates, due dates, and changes to tasks. This helps ensure that everyone is aware of their responsibilities and deadlines, promoting efficient project management.

7. **Accessibility**: Trello is available on multiple devices, including desktops, smartphones, and tablets, making it easy for team members to access their boards and collaborate on projects from anywhere.

8. **Scalability**: Trello offers various features and plans suitable for different team sizes and project complexity levels. From small teams working on simple projects to large organizations managing complex initiatives, Trello can be scaled to fit your needs.

Project Management made easy...

15.10 Asana

Website: https://asana.com/

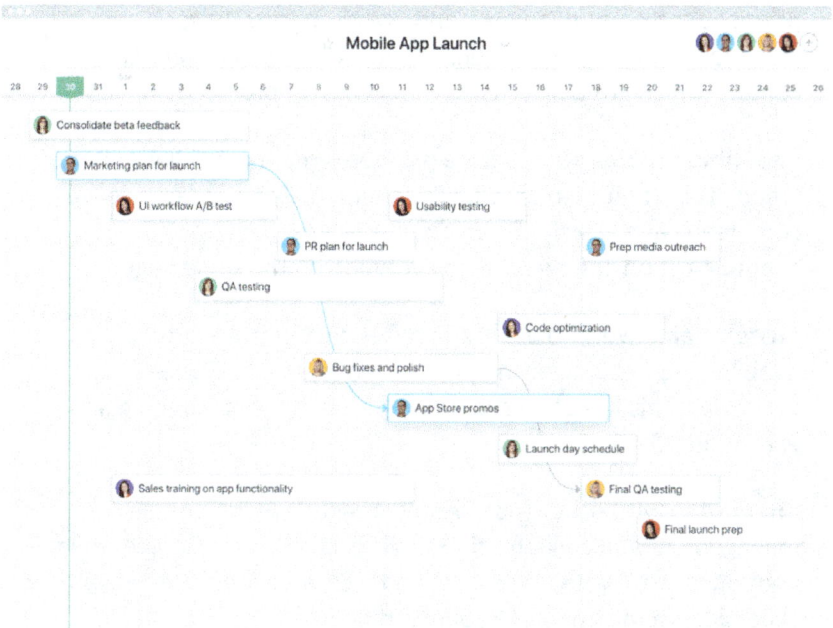

Asana is a versatile project management tool designed to help teams plan, manage, and execute work efficiently. It offers a wide range of features that enable organizations to streamline their workflows, improve collaboration, and deliver successful projects. Asana can be used by various teams and companies, regardless of the specific project management framework they follow.

Here are some reasons why Asana is an effective project management tool:

1. **Intuitive interface**: Asana's user-friendly interface allows teams to easily create, organize, and manage tasks and projects. It offers multiple views, such as list view, board view, and timeline view, to

cater to different preferences and project management methodologies.

2. **Task management**: Asana enables you to create, assign, and prioritize tasks, set deadlines, and track progress. Its task management features help ensure efficient project execution and control, which are crucial aspects of effective project management.

3. **Real-time collaboration**: Asana promotes real-time collaboration among team members by allowing them to share updates, leave comments, and attach files to tasks. This ensures clear communication and helps keep everyone on the same page.

4. **Customizable workflows**: Asana offers customizable workflows, enabling teams to tailor the platform to their specific needs and processes. This flexibility supports efficient project planning and execution.

5. **Integration with other tools**: Asana integrates with popular project management and collaboration tools, such as Slack, Google Drive, and Microsoft Teams, which can enhance your project management capabilities and streamline your workflow.

6. **Reporting and analytics**: Asana provides reporting and analytics features that help you analyse project performance, identify trends, and share insights with stakeholders. This supports data-driven decision-making and ensures project success.

7. **Scalability**: Asana offers various features and plans suitable for different team sizes and project complexity levels. From small teams working on simple projects to large organizations managing complex initiatives, Asana can be scaled to fit your needs.

8. **Accessibility**: Asana is available on multiple devices, including desktops, smartphones, and tablets, making it easy for team members to access their tasks and collaborate on projects from anywhere.

16 Building a Career in Project Management

According to figures from Project Management Institute (PMI) in their 2021 Talent Gap Report, the global economy will need 25 million new project professionals by 2030, and closing this gap will require 2.3 million people to enter project management-oriented employment (PMOE) every year just to keep up with demand.

Building a career in project management is a worthwhile approach for several reasons when beginning your professional career. Developing a strong project management skill set offers numerous benefits to business professionals, including:

1. **Broad applicability**: Project management skills are valuable across various industries and sectors, ranging from construction and technology to healthcare and finance. As a project manager, you'll have the opportunity to work in diverse fields, which can lead to a dynamic and fulfilling career.

2. **Transferable skills**: Project management involves a wide range of skills, such as communication, leadership, problem-solving, time management, and risk management. These skills are transferable and can be applied to numerous other roles, making you a versatile and valuable asset in any organisation.

3. **Career progression**: Project management offers a clear path for career advancement. As you gain experience and develop your skills, you can move into more senior roles, such as program manager, portfolio manager, or director of operations. These positions often come with increased responsibilities, higher salaries, and greater opportunities for professional growth.

4. **Networking opportunities**: Working as a project manager allows you to interact with diverse stakeholders, including clients, suppliers, and team members from various departments. This

exposure can help you build a strong professional network, which is essential for career growth and discovering new opportunities.

5. **Job satisfaction**: Project management provides a unique sense of accomplishment. As a project manager, you'll oversee projects from inception to completion, ensuring that goals are achieved on time and within budget. This responsibility and the ability to make a tangible impact on the organisation can lead to high levels of job satisfaction and personal fulfilment.

6. **High demand**: As businesses continue to evolve and face new challenges, the demand for skilled project managers remains strong. Companies recognise the importance of effective project management to achieve their strategic objectives and deliver successful projects. This ongoing demand can result in increased job security and a wide range of job opportunities for project management professionals.

7. **Opportunities for professional development**: There are numerous certifications, courses, and workshops available for project managers to enhance their skills and knowledge, such as Project Management Professional (PMP), PRINCE2, and Agile certifications. Pursuing these qualifications can improve your marketability and help you stay current in the field.

8. **Competitive salary**: Project managers often enjoy competitive salaries due to their specialised skill set and the impact they have on an organisation's success. As you progress in your career and take on larger or more complex projects, your earning potential is likely to increase.

9. **Global opportunities**: Project management skills are in demand worldwide, making it possible for professionals to pursue international career opportunities. This can open up the possibility of working in different countries and experiencing new cultures, further enriching your professional and personal life.

16.1 Qualifications and certifications

There are several different professional bodies around the world that offer qualifications and certifications for project managers. Here are a few examples:

1. **Project Management Institute** (PMI): This is one of the most well-known and respected professional bodies for project managers. They offer several certifications, including the Project Management Professional (PMP) certification, which is recognized globally.

2. **International Project Management Association** (IPMA): This is another global organization that offers certification for project managers. They have a four-level certification system, with Level D being the entry-level certification.

3. **Association for Project Management** (APM): This is the largest professional body for project managers in the UK. They offer several certifications, including the APM Project Management Qualification (PMQ), which is equivalent to IPMA Level D.

4. **PRINCE2**: This is a project management methodology developed by the UK government. It has become widely adopted around the world, and there are several certification levels available, including Foundation and Practitioner.

5. **Agile Alliance**: This is a non-profit organization that promotes Agile methodologies, including Agile project management. They offer several certifications, including the Certified Scrum Master (CSM) certification, which is focused on Scrum project management.

It's important to note that these certifications and qualifications are not mandatory for project managers, but they can be a valuable way to demonstrate your knowledge and expertise in the field.

16.2 Networking

It's often been said the project managers don't do, they help make sure things get done. One of the project managers best tools is their personal network and working actively to develop your personal network is a key and critical way of building up your credibility and effectiveness as a project manager. Here are 10 ways to do that:

1. **Attend industry events**: Conferences, seminars, and meetups are great opportunities to meet other project managers and learn about the latest trends and best practices in the industry.

2. **Join a professional association**: There are many professional associations for project managers, such as the Project Management Institute (PMI), Association for Project Management (APM), and International Project Management Association (IPMA). Joining a professional association can provide access to networking events, online forums, and other resources.

3. **Participate in online communities**: There are many online communities for project managers, such as LinkedIn groups, forums, and social media groups. Participating in these communities can provide opportunities to connect with other project managers and share knowledge and experiences.

4. **Collaborate with other project managers**: Seek out opportunities to collaborate with other project managers, whether it's through joint projects or mentoring relationships.

5. **Attend training and certification courses**: Training and certification courses can be a great way to meet other project managers and build your skills and knowledge in the field.

6. **Volunteer for industry events**: Volunteering for industry events can provide opportunities to meet other project managers and gain valuable experience.

7. **Participate in hackathons** or other innovation events: These events provide opportunities to work with other project managers and solve real-world problems.

8. **Start a blog or podcast**: Creating content related to project management can help you build your personal brand and connect with others in the industry.

9. **Engage with project management thought leaders**: Follow and engage with project management thought leaders on social media or attend their speaking engagements.

10. **Attend company events and meetups**: Many companies hold internal events or meetups for their project managers. Attending these events can help you build relationships with colleagues and other professionals in your industry.

Remember, networking is all about building relationships and adding value to others. Focus on finding ways to contribute to the project management profession and you'll be well on your way to building a strong professional network.

16.3 Tips for landing your first project management job

If you're looking for your first project management job, it can seem like a really difficult task to land a project management role. However, there are a good number of ways that you can make yourself seem more attractive to employers and here are a few ideas to help you along the way.

1. **Start with an entry-level position**: Consider starting in a role that will provide you with exposure to project management, such as a project coordinator or assistant role. Few people get their first job with the project manager title, but you can gain a lot of experience in jobs with different titles nonetheless.

2. **Develop your project management skills**: Look for ways to develop your skills and knowledge in project management, such as by taking courses or reading books and articles. In Ireland, I would recommend joining the Irish chapter of the PMI, which is run by committed and knowledgeable people who can give you great exposure to project management and the network of project managers.

3. **Get certified**: Consider obtaining a certification in project management, such as the Project Management Professional (PMP) certification from the Project Management Institute (PMI). Chapter 11 - Key Project Management organisations on page 181 will point you at their different websites and qualifications.

4. **Build your network**: Attend industry events, join professional associations, and participate in online communities to meet other project managers and build your network.

5. **Tailor your resume**: Customize your resume to highlight your relevant skills and experience in project management. You don't need "Project Manager" as a title to showcase such skills – leadership, self-direction, initiative, getting things done, starting

things, running a successful sideline, even doing something really well – all these show traits and qualities that companies are looking for in project managers.

6. **Be prepared for interviews**: Prepare for interviews by researching the company and the role, and practicing your responses to common interview questions. Remember, if they're interviewing you for a project management job, they want to know that you can hit the ground running, make things happen, and effectively communicate and manage stakeholders of all kinds.

7. **Showcase your accomplishments**: Provide concrete examples of how you've contributed to successful projects in your previous roles. Story-telling is your best bet here – tell stories of how you spotted an issue then did something to fix it. If you can provide measurable data on the benefits that accrued from your efforts – even better!

8. **Be willing to start small**: Consider taking on smaller projects or projects with less complexity to gain experience and build your portfolio. Charity and non-profit work can be a great way to demonstrate project management capability by running events, fundraisers, and other such projects.

9. **Demonstrate your leadership skills**: Highlight your ability to lead and motivate a team to achieve project goals.

10. **Stay up-to-date**: Stay informed on the latest trends and best practices in project management to demonstrate your commitment to the field.

17 Some recommended books on Project Management

There's a lot of good material out there on project management by some very experienced practitioners and writers so the list below is a curated set of project management texts that I found useful over the years that I've taught and studied in the subject. Each is linked on Amazon in case you want to read further.

- **A Project Manager's Book of Templates by Cynthia Snyder Dionisio**

    Amazon link: https://amzn.to/3KmBMxy

- **Project Management for Dummies by Nick Graham**

    Amazon link: https://amzn.to/3TV8by5

- **Leading Change by John Kotter**

    Amazon link:
    https://amzn.to/3TXMJsz

    Excellent book by one of the world's top authors on change, and inventor of the 8 steps of change outlined on page 144.

- **A Guide to the Project Management Body of Knowledge 7th edition**

    Amazon link:
    https://amzn.to/3lWu4Rd

- HBR Handbooks Series: Harvard Business Review Project Management Handbook: How to Launch, Lead, and Sponsor Successful Projects by Antonio Nieto-Rodriguez, Christopher Douyard, et al.

    Amazon link: https://amzn.to/3JWF0X4

- Agile Project Management: 3 Books in 1: The Complete Guide to Agile Project Management, Methodology & Software Development (Lean Methodology) by Jeffrey Ries

    Amazon link: https://amzn.to/3ZuFmdd

- **Project Management Next Generation: The Pillars for Organizational Excellence by Harold Kerzner**

    Amazon link: https://amzn.to/3M1Sq6y

    In *Project Management Next Generation: The Pillars for Organizational Excellence,* a team of world-renowned project management leaders delivers an expert discussion on project management implementation in organizations of all kinds.

- **Project Management: Achieving Competitive Advantage by Jeffrey Pino**

    Amazon link: https://amzn.to/40uxGJ7

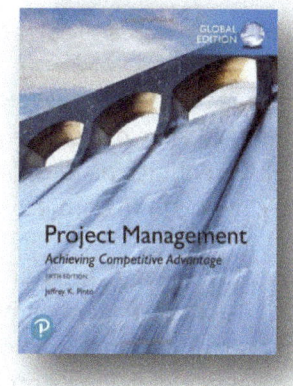

18 Conclusion

If you've made it this far, well done! Here's a brief recap of the key concepts and themes that we've covered in the book:

At its core, project management is about achieving a specific goal within a defined time frame, using a set of resources and a team of people. Projects have clear boundaries, such as a beginning and end date, a defined scope of work, and a set of deliverables.

One of the most important aspects of project management is planning. This involves defining the scope of the project, identifying the resources needed, creating a timeline, and determining how progress will be measured.

Effective communication is also crucial in project management. Project managers need to be able to communicate clearly with their team members, stakeholders, and sponsors to ensure everyone is aligned and working towards the same goal.

Project managers must also be skilled at managing risks and changes that may arise during the project. This involves identifying potential risks, creating a plan to mitigate them, and being flexible and adaptable to changes in the project scope.

There are several methodologies and frameworks that project managers can use to manage their projects. Examples include Agile, Scrum, and Kanban. These methodologies provide guidance on how to plan, execute, and deliver a project, and can be tailored to the specific needs of each project.

Finally, it's important for project managers to continually assess and improve their project management skills. This can involve seeking out training, obtaining certifications, and learning from other experienced project managers.

18.1 The future of Project Management.

As technology continues to advance and the pace of change accelerates, project management is likely to become even more important. In the future, we can expect project managers to have access to more sophisticated tools and technologies that will help them manage their projects more effectively.

18.1.1 88 million jobs

According to research conducted by the Project Management Institute (PMI), it is estimated that by 2027, employers will require nearly 88 million individuals in project management-oriented roles globally. This data suggests a significant demand for project managers in the coming years. The same report highlights that China and India will represent more than 75 percent of the total project management-oriented employment, emphasizing the importance of project managers as key contributors to productivity. You can find more information on this research in the following report: PMI Job Growth and Talent Gap report at https://www.pmi.org/learning/careers/job-growth .

18.1.2 Growth of AGILE

One of the key trends we're likely to see in the future is the continued growth of Agile and other iterative project management methodologies. As organizations seek to become more responsive to change and deliver value more quickly, Agile is becoming an increasingly popular approach. This trend is likely to continue in the future, with more and more organizations adopting Agile methodologies.

18.1.3 Artificial Intelligence

Another trend we're likely to see is the use of artificial intelligence (AI) and machine learning (ML) to help project managers manage their projects more effectively. AI and ML can help automate many routine tasks, such as scheduling and budgeting, freeing up project managers to focus on more strategic work.

With its potential to revolutionize the way we work, AI is expected to play an increasingly significant role in the future of project management. Let's explore this fascinating topic in more detail.

To begin with, it's crucial to understand what AI is and how it works. Artificial intelligence refers to the development of computer systems that can perform tasks that typically require human intelligence. These tasks may include learning, problem-solving, and decision-making. By harnessing the power of AI, project managers can improve efficiency and productivity, ultimately leading to more successful project outcomes.

One of the main ways AI can benefit project management is through automation. By automating repetitive and time-consuming tasks, project managers and their teams can focus on more critical aspects of the project. For example, AI can help with scheduling, resource allocation, and risk identification, allowing project managers to make more informed decisions and respond proactively to potential issues.

Another area where AI can make a significant impact is in data analysis. Project managers often deal with vast amounts of data, and it can be challenging to identify patterns and trends that may be crucial to project success. AI-powered tools can analyse this data more quickly and accurately than humans, enabling project managers to make better-informed decisions based on real-time insights.

Furthermore, AI can enhance communication and collaboration within project teams. By using natural language processing (NLP) and machine learning algorithms, AI can analyse team members' interactions, identify communication gaps, and even suggest ways to improve collaboration. This can help project managers maintain a more cohesive and effective team, ultimately leading to better project outcomes.

Predictive analytics is another area where AI can be a game-changer in project management. By analysing historical data and identifying patterns, AI can help project managers forecast potential risks and issues before they become significant problems. This allows project teams to proactively address these concerns, reducing the likelihood of project delays or failures.

AI can also aid in the decision-making process by providing project managers with valuable insights and recommendations based on data analysis. This can help project managers make more informed decisions, as AI can weigh multiple factors and present the best possible options for achieving project success.

Lastly, AI-powered tools can help project managers with continuous improvement. By collecting and analysing data from completed projects, AI can identify areas where processes can be optimized, helping project teams refine their approach and achieve better results in the future.

18.1.4 Developments in certifications

In addition to technology, we can also expect to see changes in the way project managers are trained and certified. As the profession becomes more specialized, we may see the emergence of new certifications and training programs that are tailored to specific industries or project types.

While it's impossible to predict the exact nature of these changes, we can make some educated guesses about the future of project management certifications and training.

1. **Greater emphasis on digital skills**: With the increasing reliance on technology and digital tools in project management, future certifications and training programs will likely place a stronger focus on developing digital skills. This includes proficiency in project management software, data analytics, and collaboration tools, as

well as an understanding of emerging technologies like artificial intelligence and machine learning.

2. **Agile methodologies and hybrid approaches**: As organizations continue to adopt agile methodologies, certifications and training programs will need to adapt and incorporate these principles. This may include a greater focus on agile project management techniques, as well as hybrid approaches that combine traditional and agile methodologies to cater to different project requirements.

3. **Focus on soft skills**: As project management becomes more complex, soft skills like leadership, communication, and problem-solving are increasingly important for project managers. Future certifications and training programs may place a higher emphasis on developing these skills, which can help project managers effectively lead diverse teams and navigate complex project environments.

4. **Cross-disciplinary knowledge**: Projects often involve collaboration across multiple disciplines, and having a broader understanding of different fields can be beneficial for project managers. Future certifications and training programs may include elements from other disciplines, such as finance, marketing, or engineering, to provide project managers with a more holistic understanding of project requirements and potential challenges.

5. **Emphasis on sustainability and social responsibility**: As organizations become more conscious of their environmental and social impact, project managers will need to consider these factors in their decision-making. Future certifications and training programs may incorporate sustainability and social responsibility concepts, equipping project managers with the knowledge and skills to make more responsible choices in their projects.

6. **Increased use of virtual and online training**: The ongoing trend toward remote work and digital communication is likely to influence the way project management training is delivered. We can expect to

see an increase in virtual and online training options, making it more accessible for individuals worldwide and allowing for more flexible learning experiences.

7. **Continuous learning and upskilling**: The rapidly changing nature of the project management profession means that project managers must continually update their skills and knowledge. Future certifications and training programs may place a greater emphasis on lifelong learning and ongoing professional development, encouraging project managers to stay current with industry trends and best practices.

18.1.5 Managing distributed teams

One of the biggest challenges facing project managers in the future will be the need to manage teams that are increasingly global and diverse. As more organizations adopt remote work and embrace diversity, project managers will need to develop new skills and approaches to manage teams effectively.

18.1.6 New roles and specialities

Finally, we can expect project management to continue to evolve as a profession. As the field matures, we may see the emergence of new roles and specialties, such as project portfolio managers, program managers, and project management office (PMO) directors.

Overall, the future of project management looks bright. As technology continues to advance and organizations seek to become more agile and responsive to change, project managers will play an increasingly important role in helping organizations develop and grow.

19 Index

3

3 Yes's and a No conversation 56
3 Yes's then a No 153

4

4-box approach 165

7

7 Habits 51
7 types of waste 223

A

AAR 171
Acceptance Criteria 208, 226
acceptance process 174
accountability 152
Accountability 36
ADHD 65
adjustable schedules 68
Affinity Diagram 218
After Action Report 171
After Action Review 170
age 62
Agile 29, 30, 205, 208, 226
Agile Alliance 191, 207, 238
Agile Manifesto 205, 208, 226
Agile methodologies 191
Allocate resources 104
American Society for Quality... 136, 217
Analyse 215, 216
APM 189
Artificial Intelligence 305
Asana 251, 270, 291
ASQ 136, 217

Assess Risks 160
assistive technology 66
Association for Project Management
.... 189
Atlassian 289
attention to detail 65
audits and reviews 124
Authoritarian leadership 259
autism 65
automation 306

B

BAC 124
Backlog 208, 226, 239
Backlog Grooming 208, 226
Baseline 30
begin with the end in mind 51
Behavioural competences 195
bell shaped curve 220
Big Dig 53
Black Belt 218
Boston Central Artery/Tunnel Project
.... 53
Bruce Williams 218
budget 53, 82, 94
Budget at Completion 124
build momentum 147
Burj Khalifa Hotel 163
Burndown Chart 208, 227
Burnup Chart 209, 227
Business Analysis 156
business case 78
buy-in and commitment 149

C

Canva 14

CAPM	188
cash flow	122
Cash Flow Management	122
cathedral	268
Cause-and-Effect Diagram	218
Celebrate Success	132
Celebrating achievements	180
Certified Associate in Project Management	188
Certified Project Management Associate	196
Certified Project Manager	196
Certified Projects Director	196
Certified Senior Project Manager	196
Change Control	30
Change Control Process	153
Change Management	124, 142, 246
Change Request	30
Change requests	153
change-ready culture	*See*
changing requirements	207
ChatGPT	14, 15
clear expectations	62
ClickUp	117, 270, 282
Closure Checklist	175
Collaboration	39
collaborative editing	251
commitment	149
commitment bias	158
Communicate Magazine	139
communication goals	138
Communication Management	138
communication plan	94
Communications Plan	138
Compliance with regulations	64
Concept Development	156
Conflict	132, 245
Conflict Management	266
Confluence	289
Constraint	30
constraints	51
Consultative Discussions	149
Contextual competences	195
contingency fund	122

contingency plans	150
Continuous Deployment	209, 227
continuous improvement	40, 220
Continuous improvement	235, 239
continuous integration	214
Continuous Integration	209, 227
Continuous integration and testing	29
continuous refactoring	192
Control	215
Control Chart	218
Control Phase	218
Control Plan	218
CoPilot	14
Corporate social responsibility	43
Cost	53
Cost overruns	123
Cost Performance Index	123
cost savings	44
Cost savings	236
Cost Variance	123
Could-haves	229
CPI	123
Craig Gygi	218
Create Flow	223
critical path	115
Critical Path	30
Critical to Quality	219
Cross-functional Team	209, 227
CSR	43
CTQ	219
culture of accountability	152
Currency fluctuations	123
currency hedging strategies	123
Customer feedback	29
Customer satisfaction	236
Customers	22
CV	123
Cycle Time	239

D

Daily Stand-up	193, 209, 227
Daily stand-up meetings	29
dashboards	164

Data-driven decision making 235
debriefing session 171
Defects 224
Define 215, 216
Define Value 223
defining the project 51
Definition of Done 209, 228
Delayed Decisions 245
Delegative leadership 259
Deliverable 30
deliverables 52
Deliverables Acceptance 174
Dependency 30
Design 216
Develop Risk Responses 160
Developing the business case 78
different perspectives 39
discrepancies 122
discrimination 62
diverse perspectives 65, 149
diverse thinking styles 66
diversity 63
DMADV 216, 220
DMAIC 215, 219
Drea Zigarmi 256
Drea Zigarmi: 256
Duplication of efforts 250
dyslexia 65
dyspraxia 65

E

Earned Value Management 30
ECCSR Framework 35
EDI 61
EDI Maturity Model 69
EDI Perception Survey 69
EDI Policy 69
EDI Policy and Data Checklist 70
EDI Vision Statement 69
effective decision-making 57
elimination of waste 222
embed the changes 148
Emotional Intelligence 144

emotional reactions 143
empathy 143
Empathy 144
End users 22
Engaging stakeholders 150
Epic 209, 228
equality and inclusion 61
Equality, Diversity, and Inclusion 61
Eric Ries 225
error-proofing 221
Establish Pull 223
Estimating Costs 121
ethical compass 36
Ethics 87
ethnicity 62
evaluating alternatives 78
Evaluation 177
evidence-based reasoning 80
EVM 30
Excess inventory 224
exchange rate fluctuations 123
Executive summary 79
Expectation Management 246
expenses 122
eXtreme Programming 214, 234

F

Failure Modes and Effects Analysis . 220
fairness 36
feasibility 51
Feasibility Study 75
Feature 210, 228
feedback loops 62
Finances 121
financial analysis 75
Financial Controls 124
Financial decision-making 124
Financial policies and procedures .. 124
Financial reporting 122
financial requirements 82
flexible working hours 66
Flow 222
FMEA 220

Focus on customer needs 235
formal acceptance document 174
forming-storming-norming-performing
.... 263
Funding disruptions 123

G

Gannter 276
Gantt chart 115
Gantt Chart 30
Gantt chart tools 116
Gantter 269
gender 62
Goleman 144
Google 113
Google Calendar 277
Google Drive 277
Google Glass 113
governance structures 195
Green Belt 220
GRI 92, 169
guiding coalition 147

H

Harvard Business Review 133, 139
HBR 140
Henry Gantt 115
High Line in New York City 129
Histogram 220
honesty 36
Hurricane Katrina recovery 169

I

Idea Generation 156
Idea Screening 156
Identify potential risks 106
Identify Risks 160
impact 110
implementation process 149
Improve 215
improve quality 215

Inappropriate processing 224
Inclusion 67
Inclusive recruitment 65
Increased Risk 243
Increment 194
incremental improvements 220
Ineffective Communication 249
initiation 51
innovation 39
Innovative teaching with AI: Creative approaches to enhancing learning in education 17
instant messaging 251
Institute change 148
Institute of Project Management ... 197
integrity 36
Interface 45
International Organization for
   Standardization 136
International Project Management
   Association 195
Invoicing and collections 122
IPM 197
IPMA 195
Iron Triangle 53
Irrational escalation of commitment
.... 158
iSix Sigma 217
ISO 136
Issue 31
issues and concerns 149
Iteration 210, 228
iterative development 191, 193

J

James C. Hunter 258
Jeffrey Liker 225
Jira 289

K

Kaizen 220, 239
Kanban 210, 228, 237, 239

Kanban Board 239
Kanban Card 239
Kanban University 238
Kanbanize 237
Ken Blanchard 256
Key Performance Indicator 220
key performance indicators 80
Kickoff Meeting 31
Knowledge Transfer 178
Kotter International 148
Kotter's 8 steps of change 146
KPI 220
KPIs 80
Kurt Lewin 259

L

Lack of collaboration 250
Larry C. Spears 258
Launch 157
LCI 198
Lead Time 239
leadership 144
Leadership 252
leadership styles 259
Lean 220, 228
LEAN 222
Lean assembly 198
Lean Construction Institute 198
Lean design 198
Lean Enterprise Institute 225
LEAN Production 225
Lean Project Delivery System 198
Lean Six Sigma 235
Lean Six Sigma for Dummies 236
Lean Six Sigma Institute 236
Lean supply 198
Lean-Agile 210, 229
LeanKit 237
legal issues 87
legal requirements 62
Lessons Learned 31
Lessons Learned Review 170
Level A 196

Level B 196
Level C 196
Level D 196
Levelling 32
Lewin's Leadership Styles Framework
.... 260
Licensing and permits 121
likelihood 110
LinkedIn 2
Little's Law 240
London 2012 Olympics 129
LPDS 198
LucidChart 101, 102

M

MacBook Air 14
machine learning algorithms 306
Magic Write 14
Manage costs 106
Managing Successful Projects with
  PRINCE2 20
Map the Value Stream 223
market analysis 75
market trends 123
Mary-Jane Jensen 263
Master Black Belt 220
MBB 220
Measure 215, 216
metrics 80
micro culture 61
Microsoft Excel 117
Microsoft Planner 269, 274
Microsoft Project 269, 272
Microsoft Teams 251
Microsoft Visio 100
Microsoft Word 14
Milestone 31, 229
milestones 82
Minimum Viable Product 210, 229
Miscommunication 250
Missed Deliverables 243
Missed Objectives 245
Mission Zero 45

Mitigate risks 106	Paul Hersey 256
mitigation strategies 81	Payment scheduling..................... 122
Monday.com 270, 286	Perfection 222
Monitor and evaluate progress 63	performance 53
Monitor Quality Performance 135	performance metrics 152
Monitor Risks 160	Performance Metrics..................... 123
MoSCoW 229	**performance monitoring framework**
Motivation............................. 144, 267	 80
Motorola 215	perspectives 149
MS Teams 275	PERT... 229
MS Word Outline View 98	PESTEL 108
Must-haves 229	*Picture perfect* 18
MVP 210, 229	Planning Poker........................210, 229
	PlanView.. 237
N	Plus One Education series 17
	PMBOK 31, 53, 187, 188, 189, 197, 230, 252, 258, 260
NASA Mars Rover............................ 163	PMI 31, 53, 58, 133, 136, 187, 188, 197, 202, 230, 258, 261, 262, 266, 272, 273, 276, 277, 278, 279, 280, 281, 282, 283, 284, 295, 296, 298, 305
natural language processing........... 306	
Neurodiversity 65	
neurotypical...................................... 66	
new products 216	
NLP... 306	PMLC 26
	PMO...31, 309
O	PMP 188
	Poka-Yoke....................................... 221
objectives.. 51	Poor communication 249
open communication 37	Poor Resource Planning................. 247
OpenProject 270, 280	**positive work culture** 40
open-source software..................... 281	PPM 32
optimization of processes.............. 222	Predictive analytics........................ 307
Outline View 98	PRINCE2 ..... 20, 160, 185, 186, 197, 295
Outlook 275	Proactive Action 149
Over-allocating Resources 247	process improvement.................... 201
Overhead..................................... 122	Product Backlog.............................. 194
Overproduction 224	Product Owner 211, 230
	Professionalism............................. 37
P	Program Evaluation and Review Technique 229
pair programming 192, 214	**project budget** 82
Pareto Chart 221	Project Charter 31, 82
Pareto Principle 221	Project Closure 167
Participative leadership 259	Project definition............................ 198
Patagonia 45	Project Development..................... 156
Patricia Zigarmi 256	Project Evaluation 177

Project Execution 126
Project initiation 51
Project Life Cycle 31
Project Management Body of
    Knowledge 31, 53, 187, 230, 260
Project Management Institute ... 31, 53,
    133, 136, 187, 202, 230, 260, 295,
    296, 298, 305
Project Management Life Cycle 26
Project management made easy 17
Project Management Office 31
Project Management organisations 183
Project Management Professional .. 188
project management templates 58
project manager 21
Project Manager............................... 32
Project Monitoring and Controlling 151
project objectives 93
Project Performance Monitoring 152
Project Planning 89
Project Portfolio Management 32
project schedule 97
Project Schedule 114
project scope 243
Project scope 51
project sponsor 22, 82
project stakeholders 22
project status on a page 165
project timeline 76, 82
project's purpose 80
ProjectManagement.com 58
ProjectManager.com 58, 133
Pull 222
Pull System 239
Pursue Perfection 223

Q

quality 53
Quality 53
quality assurance processes 53
quality control 201
Quality Control 135
quality control measures 54

Quality management 53
Quality Management . 32, 54, 135, 200,
    201
Quality Performance 135
Quality Progress Magazine 137
quality standards 53
Quality Standards 135
quick turnaround times 207

R

recommendations 171
Recommended option 79
reduce defects 215
Reduce uncertainty 106
Reduced team morale 250
Regular audits and reviews 124
regular check-ins 151
Release 211, 230
remote working options 68
removing barriers 147
reputation 43, 64
Requirements 32
Requirements gathering 29
Resource Allocation 32, 247
Resource Forecasting 248
Resource Levelling 32, 248
resource optimization 44
Resource Planning 104
resource schedule 104
resource usage 104
resources 53
results 47
retrospective 29
Retrospective 193, 211, 230
return on investment 80
Return on Investment 123
revenues 122
risk 53
Risk 32
risk analysis 75
Risk Management 32, 248
Risk Management Planning 106
risk matrix 110

risk mitigation strategies 111
Risk Monitoring and Control........... 160
Risk Register 161
risk response plan 161
Roadmap 211, 230
Robert Cooper 155
Robert K. Greenleaf 257
ROI 123
Roles and Responsibilities 131
Royal Photographic Society 180

S

schedule 53
Schedule 114
Schedule Variance 32, 123
Scheduling 32
Scope 33, 53
scope creep 57
Scope Creep 33, 243, 245
Scrum 211, 231
Scrum Alliance 193, 207
Scrum artifacts 194
Scrum events 193
Scrum Master 212, 231
Scrum roles 193
SDLC 26
Segregation of duties 124
Self-awareness 144
Self-regulation 144
sense of ownership 149
sequential approach 203
Servant Leadership 256
SharePoint 275
short-term wins 147
Should-haves 229
sign-off 174
Simon Sinek 267
Situational leadership 252, 255
Situational Leadership 255
Six Sigma 201, 215
Six Sigma for Dummies 218
Slack 251
SmartArt WBS 102

Social skills 145
software development 192
software development life cycle 26
Sprint 212, 231
Sprint Backlog 194, 212, 231
Sprint Goal 212, 231
Sprint planning 29
Sprint Planning 193, 212, 232
Sprint Retrospective 193
Sprint review 29
Sprint Review 193, 213, 232
sprints 191
Stage-Gate Process 155
Stakeholder 33
Stakeholder Analysis 246
stakeholder buy-in 80
stakeholder expectations 245
Stakeholder Expectations 139
stakeholder management 60
Stakeholders 60
Start with Why 267
Start-Stop-Continue 171
Status Meeting 33
status meetings 151
Status Report 33
Status Reporting 164
Steven Covey 51
stonemasons 267
Story Points 213, 232
strategic alignment 195
strategic objectives 80
strategic vision 147
strategy 78
Street photography – get out and do it
.... 180
Streets of Dublin 18
success criteria 80
sustain momentum 148
Sustainability 84
Sustainable practice 43
Sustainable results 42
SV 32, 123
Swimlane 240
SWOT tool 109

T

Take your time – the art and craft of long exposure photography 18
Takt Time 240
Task 33
Task Board 213, 232
Task Duration 33
Task prioritization 126
tasks 96
Team building 262
Team Building 261
Team Central 289
team management 252
team meetings 164
team members 21
team recognition 180
TeamGantt 269, 278
technical analysis 75
Technical competences .. 195
Template.net 58
templates 58
Terry Gustafson 218
test-driven development 192, 214
Testing and Validation 157
The 7 Habits of Highly Effective People 51
The Decision Lab 159
The Global Reporting Initiative . 92, 169
The Kanban Guide 238
The Lean Six Sigma Pocket Toolbook 236
The Lean Startup 225
The Six Sigma Handbook ... 236
The Toyota Way 225
Time 53
Time Estimation 33
Time Management 33
time-boxed phases 193
Timeboxing 213, 232
Toyota 222
tracking 151
Training and development ... 62
Transformational leadership 254
Transformational Leadership 254
transparent decision-making 80
Transport 224
Trello 250, 270, 289
Triple Constraint 33
Trust and Respect 131
Tuckman's team formation cycle 263

U

uncertain environments 192
Unclear Requirements 243
Under-allocating Resources 247
Unnecessary motion 224
Unnecessary Work 243
urgency 147
Use and maintenance 199
User Story 213, 233

V

value 41
Value 222
Variance Analysis 33
variances 122
Velocity 214, 233
Verify 216
video conferencing 251
Voice Control for ChatGPT ... 15
volunteer army 147

W

Waiting 224
waste reduction 44
Waterfall 33, 203
Waterfall model 27
WBS 34, 93, 96, 97, 98, 104, 121
WebChatGPT 15
WIP 34, 214, 233, 237, 239
WIP limit 214
WIP limits 233
Won't-haves 229
Work Breakdown Structure 34, 96, 121

Work in Progress 214, 233
Work In Progress 239
Work Package 34
Workflow 214, 233
Work-in-Progress 34
Wrike 59, 270, 284

X

XP 192, 214, 234

Z

Zero Bug Policy 214, 234

www.ingramcontent.com/pod-product-compliance
Lightning Source LLC
Chambersburg PA
CBHW051601230426
43668CB00013B/1934